Writers at Work

The Paragraph

Jill Singleton

CAMBRIDGE UNIVERSITY PRESS
Cambridge, New York, Melbourne, Madrid, Cape Town, Singapore, São Paulo, Delhi

Cambridge University Press
32 Avenue of the Americas, New York, NY 10013–2473, USA

www.cambridge.org
Information on this title: www.cambridge.org/9780521545228

First published 2005
7th printing 2008

Printed in the United States of America

A catalog record for this publication is available from the British Library

Library of Congress Cataloging in Publication Data
Singleton, Jill.
    Writers at work. The paragraph / Jill Singleton.
        p. cm.
    ISBN 978-0-521-54522-8 (pbk.)
        1. English language–Textbooks for foreign speakers. 2. English language – Paragraphs
    Problems, exercises, etc. I. Title: Paragraph. II. Title

ISBN 978-0-521-54522-8 paperback

Art direction and book design: Adventure House, NYC
Layout services: Page Designs International

Illustration credits: Rick Powell

Photo credits: page 2: © Alamy; page 6: © Paul Barton/Corbis, © Alamy, © GDT/Getty,
© Paul Barton/Corbis; page 20: © Joe Polillio/Getty, © Martin Barraud/Getty, © Annie
Marie Musselman/Getty, © Punchstock; page 38: © Brian Bailey/Getty, © Punchstock,
© Richard T. Nowitz/Corbis, © Justin Pumfrey/Getty; page 52: © Corbis, © Tom & Dee
Ann McCarthy/Corbis, © George Logan/Getty; page 64: © Punchstock, © Mark L.
Stephenson/Corbis, © Ariel Skelley/Corbis; page 78: © Gabe Palmer/Corbis, © Robert
Llewellyn/Alamy; page 88: © Michael Melford/Getty, © Punchstock, © Doug
Armand/Getty; page 98: © Brown W. Cannon III/Getty, © Punchstock, © Jose Luis
Pelaez Inc./Corbis; page 112: © Jeff Greenberg/Alamy, © Sean Cayton/The Image
Works, © James Cheadle/Alamy

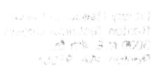

To my son Rob, with love

Table of Contents

Chapter Contents

Begin at the Beginning

CHAPTER 1 A Morning Person or a Night Person?

* The items in this column refer to the titles of the
information boxes that appear throughout the book.

CHAPTER 2 A Person Important to You

CHAPTER 3 The Weekend

CHAPTER 4 A Scary or Funny Experience

CHAPTER 5 Holidays

CHAPTER 6 Telling Stories

CHAPTER 7 A Favorite Place

CHAPTER 8 The Ideal Spouse

CHAPTER 9   What's Your Opinion?

Quick Check

Introduction

THE *WRITERS AT WORK* SERIES

The *Writers at Work* series takes high beginning to high intermediate-level writing students through a process approach to writing. The series is intended primarily for adults whose first language is not English, but it may also prove effective for younger writers or for native speakers of English who are developing their competence as independent writers in English.

Writers at Work: The Paragraph prepares high beginning to low intermediate students to write well-organized and accurate paragraphs. *Writers at Work: The Short Composition* prepares low intermediate to intermediate-level students to write well-constructed and accurate short compositions. Finally, *Writers at Work: The Essay* prepares intermediate to high intermediate students to write fully-developed essays with an introduction, body paragraphs, and a conclusion. Upon completion of the last book in the series, students will be ready for more advanced-level academic writing courses.

The approach

Competence in writing comes from knowing *how* to write as much as from knowing *what* to write. That is why the *Writers at Work* books are organized around the process of writing. They teach students about the writing process and then guide them to use it as they write. We believe that once students understand how to use the writing process in writing paragraphs, short compositions, and essays, they will gain the confidence they need to advance to more complex writing tasks.

In teaching writing to lower level students, there is always the risk of sacrificing creativity in order to achieve accuracy, or vice versa. The *Writers at Work* books guide students through the writing process in such a way that their final pieces of writing are not only expressive and rich in content, but also clear and accurate.

Chapter structure

Each chapter is divided into the following five parts:

I Getting Started

Students are stimulated to think about the topic of the chapter. They generate ideas that they can use later in their writing.

II Preparing the First Draft

Students organize, plan, and write their first draft.

ABOUT *WRITERS AT WORK: THE PARAGRAPH*

Chapter structure

Each chapter is divided into the following five parts:

I Getting Started

Students are stimulated to think about the topic of the chapter. They generate ideas that they can use later in their writing.

II Preparing the First Draft

Students organize, plan, and write their first draft.

III Revising Your Writing

In this section, students analyze sample paragraphs and compositions, learn about key elements of writing, and apply those principles in revisions of their first drafts.

IV Editing Your Writing

Students are introduced to selected aspects of grammar. They edit their writing for accurate grammar and write their final drafts.

V Following Up

Students share their writing with each other. Finally, they fill out a self-assessment form, which allows them to track their progress as writers throughout the course.

Key features

- The book begins with an introductory section, "Begin at the Beginning," which introduces students to the writing process, including its recursive nature.

- The nine chapters of the book are thematic, each one dealing with a topic of personal interest. All of the activities and exercises in a chapter relate to the theme. In this way, students can discover vocabulary to use in their own writing on the theme.

- Sample paragraphs are presented for students to analyze, revise, and edit in preparation for working on their own writing. A major goal of the text is to help students, bit by bit, to become more proficient at revising and editing their own writing.

- Systematic and cumulative instruction in paragraph construction and in building sentences is presented in a logical and manageable way.

- Student interaction is important in *Writers at Work: The Paragraph*. Throughout the book, students are carefully guided to help each other write more clearly and think more critically about writing.

- "Sharing Your Writing" activities at the end of each chapter engage students in sharing their final drafts.

- "Quick Check," an editing and grammar reference at the end of the book, introduces students to useful editing symbols and covers the most common basic writing errors. It can be used by students when editing their writing or by teachers as extra help for an individual student.

A FINAL NOTE

No writing text can encompass the great variety of activities in a writing class. In addition to the carefully sequenced writing assignments in the text, it is essential that students do a good deal of unstructured writing in order to increase their fluency and comfort in writing in English. Activities such as journals, dialogue journals, and informal letter-writing and e-mailing are vital to the growth of the students' writing ability. It is highly recommended that the teacher include such activities in the class.

Acknowledgements

I would like to express my appreciation to the many people who have made this second edition a reality. I would first like to thank all of my students at the English Language Center of Towson University for their generosity in sharing their writing and insights. I am very grateful, too, to the teachers and staff of the ELC for their continued help and support over the years. Special thanks go to Mary Jo Lindeman, teacher at the ELC, for all the time and thought she unstintingly gave to this revision.

Many thanks to the following students for graciously allowing me to use their writing in this book: Sami Al-Wehaibi, Osama Bulbul, Maria Coronado, Jeeyeon Jang, Hyung Kyu Kang, Hee Seung Lee, Shan Yih Liu, Aymeric Menargues, Myung Hwan Moon, Jin Seok Park, Jeongin Pu, Diana Rangel, Jung Youn Sim, In-Hyuk Song, Nuraputra Sudrajat, Yoji Yamada, and Shu-Hui Yang.

At Cambridge University Press, I would especially like to thank Bernard Seal, commissioning editor, whose vision and persistence turned an idea into reality. Thanks also go to the project editor, Helen Lee; and to the copyeditor, Linda LiDestri for all their help and hard work. Many thanks also to Ann Strauch, series co-author, who has been such a pleasure to work with.

Jennifer Bixby, freelance development editor, deserves special thanks for her kindness and thoughtfulness, which made our work together both pleasant and productive.

Appreciation is also due to Don Williams, the compositor, and to the designers at Adventure House for their care and hard work.

I am grateful to the following reviewers for their thoughtful criticisms and helpful suggestions: Randee Falk; Joe McVeigh; Catherine Salin, Columbus Torah Academy; and Larry Sims, University of California at Irvine, Extension.

Most of all, thank you to my husband Phil and my son Rob for your unfailing support and for keeping me from "working on the book 24/7," as Rob said.

Begin at the Beginning

You are a writer. You are a writer in your own language, and soon you will be a writer in English. In your native language, you are probably a good writer. But do you ever think about writing? Do you ever think about why or how you write? Do you ever think about how to make your writing better?

In this section, you will think about *when* you write, *why* you write, and *how* you write.

A Reasons for writing

1 Think about writing in your native language. When do you write? Do you take notes, e-mail your friends, or make a list for the grocery store? Write your answers in the chart in your native language, not in English.

When do you write?	Why do you write?

2 With your class, talk about your answers. Together, make a list of when people in your class write and why they write.

B Thoughts about writing

Answer these questions on a separate piece of paper. Then talk about your answers with a partner or with your class.

1 Is writing easy or hard for you? Do you love it or hate it? Why?

2 Do you only write when you have to, or do you sometimes write for fun?

3 What will help you become a better writer?

A Steps for writing

THE WRITING PROCESS

Most people agree that writing well is difficult in any language. But you can make writing easier if you use the writing process. In any process, you do steps in a certain order. First, you do one thing. Then, you do another thing, and after that, you do something else. Writing also follows a process. Good writers follow the steps of the writing process when they write.

Look at these pictures. They show the steps that good writers use when they write a paragraph or short composition, but they are not in the correct order. Number the pictures to show the correct order.

Step: _____

revise
(check ideas)

Step: _____

organize
ideas and
plan writing

Step: _____

write

Step: _____

edit (check
grammar)

Step: _____

get ideas

B Using the writing process

Answer these questions on a piece of paper. Then talk about your answers with a partner or with your class.

1 Do you use any of these steps when you write something for a class? Which steps do you use?

2 Good writers do not use the writing process for every kind of writing. For example, if you write a phone message, you do not revise and edit. What other kinds of writing do not need the writing process? Give several examples.

Are you ready to begin?

Life is messy. It doesn't happen step by step. The process of writing is the same way. Good writers move forward and backward between the steps. For example, when you are writing your paragraph, you may think of a better way to organize your ideas. That's good! That is how experienced writers really write. With this book, you will improve your writing by using the writing process.

A Morning Person or a Night Person?

Do you like the morning or the night better? Do you like to wake up early in the morning, or stay up late at night? Are you a morning person or a night person?

In this chapter, you will write a paragraph about the time of day that you like the best. You will tell why you like the morning or the night and what you do in the morning or at night.

A Picture this

Answer the questions about each photograph with your class or in a small group.

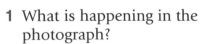

1 What is happening in the photograph?
2 How do the people in the photograph feel?
3 Do you like to do the activity in the photograph?
4 Does this usually happen at night or in the morning?

B Get ideas

BRAINSTORMING

One way to get ideas for writing is to brainstorm. *Brainstorming* means to think about a topic and write down as many ideas as possible in a list. When you brainstorm, write words or phrases. You don't need to write sentences. Some ideas will be good ones, and others will not be useful. But list all of the ideas that you can think of. Later you can choose the ideas that you want to use. The important thing when you brainstorm is to write down as many ideas as possible.

Follow these steps to get ideas for your paragraph.

1 As a class, brainstorm about the words *morning* and *night.* On the board or on a large sheet of paper, write all of the ideas in a class list. Write down words and phrases about *why you like it, what you do,* and *how you feel* about the morning and the night.

2 Now decide if you will write about the morning or the night. Circle *Morning* or *Night* in the box below.

3 Look at the class list of ideas. In the box below, copy the words that you want to use in your paragraph.

4 Add any more words that are important for your paragraph. Be sure that you have words to tell *why you like* the morning or the night, *what you do* then, and *how you feel.*

Morning / Night

A Organize your ideas

ORGANIZING IDEAS

After you brainstorm, you will have many ideas on your paper. But you are not ready to begin writing your paragraph yet. First, you need to decide which ideas to use. Will you use all of the ideas on your paper, or only some of them? Also, you need to think about the order of your ideas. Which ideas will you write about first, second, and third? When you think about and decide these things, you are *organizing* your ideas.

Circle your topic, *Morning person* or *Night person*. Then use the chart to help you organize your ideas. Write your words from the box on page 7 into the different categories. You can add more ideas.

Morning person / Night person

Why I like it	What I do	How I feel

B Plan your writing

THE MAIN IDEA

In English, each paragraph should be about only one main idea. The *main idea* is what the paragraph is about. All of the sentences in the paragraph should be about the main idea. If a sentence is about the main idea, it is a relevant sentence. *Relevant* means related to or about the main idea. If a sentence is not about the main idea, the sentence is *irrelevant* (not relevant). You should always take irrelevant sentences out of your paragraph.

Practice 1

Look at each group of words and phrases about a main idea. Put an X next to the irrelevant word or phrase. The first one is done for you.

1 morning

- _____ **a** breakfast
- __X__ **b** go dancing
- _____ **c** read the paper
- _____ **d** new day

2 afternoon

- _____ **a** lunch
- _____ **b** work
- _____ **c** classes
- _____ **d** moon

3 evening

- _____ **a** dinner
- _____ **b** watch the news
- _____ **c** pretty sunrise
- _____ **d** wash dishes

4 night

- _____ **a** sunshine
- _____ **b** do homework
- _____ **c** relax
- _____ **d** call family and friends

Practice 2

In each group of sentences below, one of the sentences is irrelevant. Put an X next to the irrelevant sentence.

1 _____ **a** It is quiet and peaceful early in the morning.

_____ **b** I like the fresh feeling in the air.

_____ **c** I go jogging then because there are few cars on the roads.

_____ **d** Some people are tired and cranky in the morning.

2 _____ **a** My cat loves the night, of course.

_____ **b** He goes hunting for mice then.

_____ **c** Dead mice make me sick.

_____ **d** He also fights with other cats at night.

3 _____ **a** My sister can't keep her eyes open after ten at night.

_____ **b** I think the best time of the day is after midnight.

_____ **c** I love to stay up and watch old movies on TV.

_____ **d** It is also a good time to read and listen to music.

4 _____ **a** I like to have a snack and read the newspaper.

_____ **b** My brother gets home at 4:30.

_____ **c** Late afternoon is my favorite time of day.

_____ **d** I usually relax for an hour.

Your turn ⌒

Follow these steps to check for any irrelevant ideas in your chart on page 8.

1 Are all of your ideas relevant to your main idea? If an idea is irrelevant (not relevant), cross it out (~~irrelevant idea~~).

2 Look at all your relevant ideas. Do you want to use them all? Cross out any ideas that you don't want to use.

3 Do you have any new ideas? Add any new ideas to your chart.

4 Now look at your chart and think about writing a paragraph with your ideas. Decide what idea you want to write about first, second, third, and so on. Number your ideas.

C Write the first draft

> **THE FIRST DRAFT**
>
> After you plan your writing, you are ready to write your paragraph for the first time. The first time you write a paragraph, it is called the *first draft*. Get comfortable and relax! In the first draft, try to write your ideas in an interesting way, and don't worry about making mistakes. Remember, after you write your paragraph, you will check it two times (revising and editing). You will have plenty of time to make it better.

Write the first draft of your paragraph. Be sure to write about *why you like* the morning or the night, *what you do* then, and *how you feel* then. Use your chart to help you.

III REVISING YOUR WRITING

> **REVISING**
>
> After you write your paragraph, you will need to revise it. *Revise* means to check your ideas. Before you wrote your first draft, you planned your writing. Did you follow your plan? Or did you change your plan while you wrote? Ask yourself, "Did I say what I wanted to say?" *Revise* does not mean check your grammar. You will have time to do that after you revise.

A Analyze a paragraph

Read a student's first draft on the next page. It has not been revised or edited yet. It may have mistakes in organization and grammar. Answer the following questions. Then talk about your answers with your class.

1 What do you like about this paragraph?

2 Is the paragraph about one main idea?

3 Are all of the sentences relevant to the main idea? Are there any irrelevant sentences?

Night

Night is the best time for me. In the evening. I call my friends. We go to a club. And have a good time. My brother doesn't like to come with us. He stays home and studies. My friends and I dance and talk for a long time. We drink coffee and smoke. My brother thinks I should not smoke. He says I will kill myself with cigarettes. Then, we each go to our own home. At home, I drink one more cup of coffee. And listen to the music of silence. I look out the window. How beautiful is the moon! Some men have walked on it. I look at the moon. Think about my future. The clock says midnight. Everything silent, serene, and perfect. I feel like midnight, too.

B Revise your writing

REVISING WITH A PARTNER

When you revise your first draft, it is a good idea to get help from a classmate. Another reader can tell you if they can easily understand your paragraph. At this time, do not check grammar.

Exchange the first draft of your paragraph with a partner. Read your partner's paragraph, and answer these questions about it.

1 What do you like about your partner's paragraph? Put a star next to any ideas or sentences that you like.
2 Read the paragraph again. Do all of the sentences relate to the main idea? Does the paragraph have any irrelevant sentences? If you think a sentence is irrelevant, put parentheses ( ) around it.

Your turn 〰

Get your paragraph back from your partner. Reread your own paragraph, and answer these questions.

1 Did your partner find any irrelevant sentences? Do you agree that the sentences are irrelevant? If you agree, cross out the irrelevant sentences.
2 Are there any other irrelevant sentences that your partner did not find?
3 Check your chart on page 8. Did you write about everything that you wanted to write about? Do you want to add anything more to your paragraph?

C Write the second draft

Rewrite your paragraph and make any changes that you need. Write a title at the top of your paragraph.

A Focus on sentence grammar

EDITING

After you revise the ideas in your paragraph, you are ready to edit it. *Edit* means to check the grammar in your writing. It is important to revise your ideas first and then edit your grammar. If you revise first, you will not waste your time editing irrelevant sentences.

Practice 3

Some of the sentences from the paragraph "Night" on page 11 do not have correct sentence grammar. They make the paragraph difficult to read. Read these sentences from the paragraph. Write *C* for correct or *I* for incorrect next to each sentence. You will check your answers later, in *Practice 6* on page 14.

_____ **1** Night is the best time for me.

_____ **2** In the evening.

_____ **3** I call my friends.

_____ **4** We go to a club.

_____ **5** And have a good time.

_____ **6** Everything silent, serene, and perfect.

SIMPLE SENTENCES

In English, every sentence must have a subject and a verb. A sentence with a subject and a verb is called a *simple sentence*.

A *subject* tells who or what the sentence is about. A simple sentence can have more than one subject.

S
Jackie hates the morning.

S
She never gets up or speaks to anyone before nine o'clock.

              S   S
Every morning, her mother and father wake up at six o'clock.

S
They can't understand Jackie.

A *verb* tells what the subject is or does. A simple sentence can have more than one verb.

              V

Jackie <u>hates</u> the morning.

          V   V

She never <u>gets up</u> or <u>speaks</u> to anyone before nine o'clock.

                              V

Every morning, her mother and father <u>wake up</u> at six o'clock.

            V

They <u>can't understand</u> Jackie.

Practice 4

Which of these words can be subjects and which words can be verbs? Write the words in the correct column in the chart.

| I | aunt and uncle | like | eats | night | roommate |
| am | newspaper | snore | she | is | thinks |

Subjects	Verbs

Practice 5

Underline the subjects and circle verbs in these sentences. Write *S* for subject and *V* for verb. The first sentence is done for you.

     S   *V*

1 <u>Dave</u> (likes) afternoons the best.

2 He gets up early in the morning for his classes.

3 His eyes often close in his 8 A.M. class.

4 At 12:30, he meets his friends and eats lunch with them.

5 Dave and his friends play soccer in the afternoon.

6 Soccer is their favorite sport.

7 After soccer, everyone has something to drink and talks about the game.

8 Then, Dave goes home for dinner.

Practice 6

Look back at *Practice 3* on page 12. Does every sentence have a subject and a verb? Check your answers with your class.

Practice 7

Put these words in the right order to make simple sentences. Sometimes there are several right answers. You only need to write one right answer. Remember to begin each sentence with a capital letter and to put a period at the end of each sentence. The first sentence is done for you.

1 at / get up / 7:30 / I
   I get up at 7:30.
   _____

2 morning / I / in / the / go / classes / to
   _____

3 order / at / pizza / my / roommate / noon / I / and
   _____

4 I / bed / in / on / study / afternoon / the / my / usually
   _____

5 in / the / my / visit / me / evening / friends
   _____

6 we / and / listen / talk / to / music
   _____

7 leave / at / my / friends / 11:30
   _____

8 light / turn / out / I / at / midnight / my
   _____

Practice 8

The paragraph at the top of the next page has no punctuation or capital letters to show sentences. Decide where the sentences begin and end. Put a capital letter at the beginning of each sentence and a period at the end. All of the sentences are simple sentences. The first sentence has been done for you.

Daylight Saving Time

/In the United States, we have daylight saving time for half of the year. in late spring, we put our clocks forward one hour then we have an extra hour of daylight every day farmers are happy for an extra hour to work in the fields children have more time to play outside their parents are happy about that adults have time to play sports after work everyone likes the extra daylight in the summer

Practice 9

Read the following paragraph. Notice that the writer took out all the irrelevant sentences from the first draft of this paragraph on page 11. With your class, decide which sentences are correct and which are not. Then write a corrected version of the paragraph.

Night

Night is the best time for me. In the evening. I call my friends. We go to a club. And have a good time. My friends and I dance and talk for a long time. We drink coffee and smoke. Then, we each go to our own home. At home, I drink one more cup of coffee. And listen to the music of silence. I look out the window. How beautiful is the moon! I look at the moon. Think about my future. The clock says midnight. Everything silent, serene, and perfect. I feel like midnight, too.

Practice 10

Look at this paragraph about the morning. Decide which sentences are correct and which are not. Then write a corrected version of the paragraph.

In the Morning

I love the early morning! I listen to the songs of the birds. The sun's rays enter my room. Through the window. I always leave the curtains open for the morning sun. I usually walk. In the early morning. I energetic and peaceful. My day starts happy. Then, I cook my breakfast. And take a shower. I begin to study. Also listen to music because I feel happy. In the morning. Time passes very fast. I think the morning is more productive than the night.

B Edit your writing

Use the *Editing Checklist* below to edit your second draft. Follow these steps.

1 Underline all of the subjects in your sentences. Circle all of the verbs.

2 Read your paragraph several times. Using the *Editing Checklist*, look for only one kind of mistake each time you read your paragraph. For example, the first time you read your paragraph, ask yourself, "Does every sentence have a subject and a verb?" The next time you read it, look for a different kind of mistake.

3 Use *Quick Check* on pages 123–140 to help you fix your mistakes.

EDITING CHECKLIST ☑

Look at each sentence.

☐ **1** Does every sentence have a subject and a verb?

Look at each verb.

☐ **2** Do all of the verbs agree with their subjects?

☐ **3** Are all of the verbs the correct tense?

☐ **4** Are all of the verbs the correct form?

Look at the punctuation and capitalization.

☐ **5** Does each sentence begin with a capital letter?

☐ **6** Does each sentence end with the correct punctuation?

Look at the words.

☐ **7** Is each word spelled correctly?

C Write the final draft

Write your final draft, including your changes and corrections. Use correct format.

A Share your writing

Follow these steps to share your writing.

1 Put everyone's papers on desks or tables in the classroom.
2 Move around the room and read your classmates' paragraphs.
3 Do you have more morning people or night people in your class?

B Check your progress

After you get your paragraph back from your teacher, complete the *Progress Check* below.

PROGRESS CHECK

Date: _____

Paragraph title: _____

Things I did well in this paragraph:

_____

_____

_____

Things I need to work on in my next paragraph:

_____

_____

_____

A Person Important to You

"No man is an island." John Donne, a famous English writer, wrote this line. What do you think it means?

Everyone needs other people. Think about the important people in your life. Whom do you love and admire? Is it a family member, a friend, a teacher, or someone else?

In this chapter, you will write a paragraph about someone important to you.

A Picture this

Answer the questions about each photograph with your class or in a small group.

1 What can you guess about this person? For example, can you guess the person's age or occupation? Can you guess if the person is married or single?
2 How can you describe the person's appearance?

B Get ideas

To prepare for writing, study these words for describing personality.

Describing personality

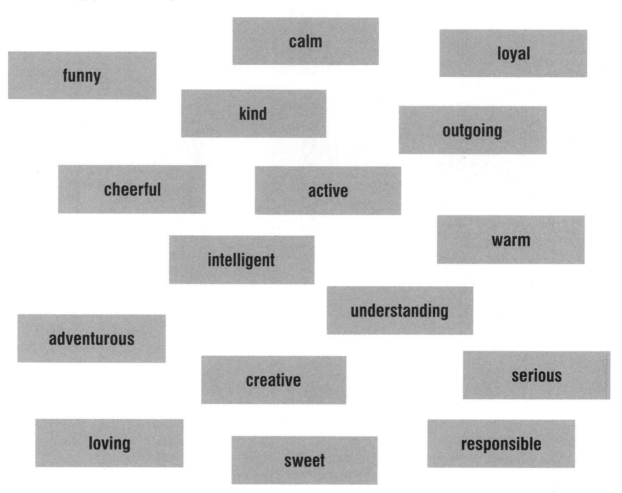

Your turn ∿

Write four words that describe your personality and four words that describe a family member's personality.

My personality   My _____'s personality

_____   _____

_____   _____

_____   _____

_____   _____

To prepare for writing, study these words for describing people.

Describing appearance

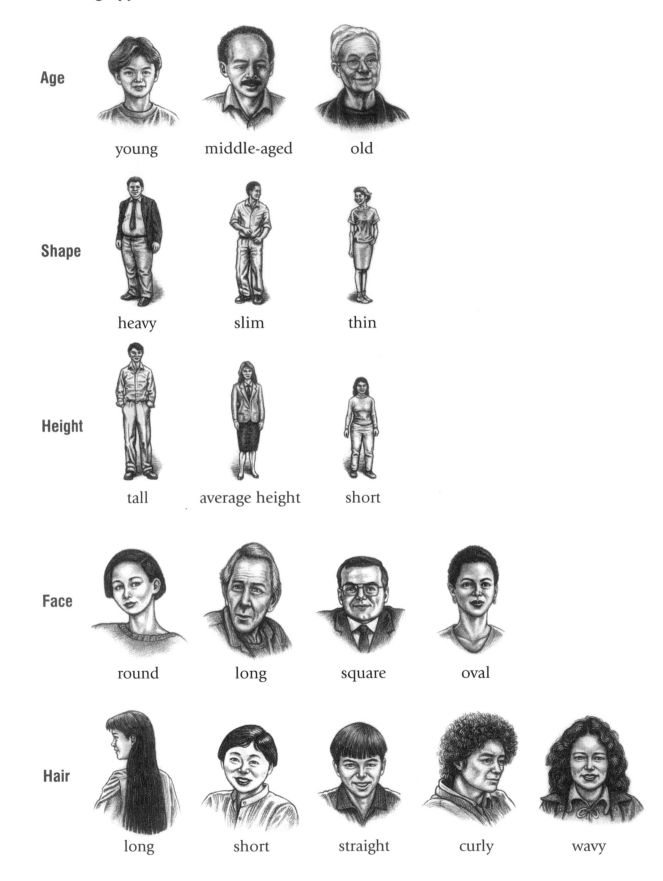

Age
young   middle-aged   old

Shape
heavy   slim   thin

Height
tall   average height   short

Face
round   long   square   oval

Hair
long   short   straight   curly   wavy

Eyes   dark brown   light brown   blue   green   gray

Women

Appearance

attractive/beautiful   unattractive/ugly

Men

Appearance

attractive/handsome   unattractive/ugly

Features

beard   moustache

Your turn ↶

Write four words that describe your appearance and four words that describe a partner's appearance. When you finish, compare lists with your partner. How are they the same or different?

My appearance   My partner's appearance

_____   _____

_____   _____

_____   _____

_____   _____

BRAINSTORMING

Brainstorming is a good way to get ideas for writing. When you brainstorm, try to list as many ideas as possible. Don't worry if it's a good idea or a bad idea. Write down all of your ideas.

For example, Sara wanted to write about her younger brother, Adam. To get ideas for her paragraph, she wrote this list of ideas.

Adam

I miss him!	goes to school every day	smart
younger brother	I had his teacher before.	follows my teenage brother around
10 years old	loves school	drives him crazy
a little heavy	cheerful	laughs a lot
short for his age	sweet	curly dark brown hair
the youngest	brown eyes	plays soccer after school
2 brothers, 1 sister	I wrote to him yesterday.	

Your turn ↶

Follow these steps to brainstorm ideas about a person important to you.

1 Make a list of four or five people who are important to you.
2 Circle the name of the person you want to write about.
3 Brainstorm as many words or phrases as you can about that person. Use the vocabulary on pages 21–23 to help you describe the person.

Name of person: _____

II PREPARING THE FIRST DRAFT

A Organize your ideas

ORGANIZING BY CATEGORY

After you brainstorm, you will need to organize your ideas. One way to organize ideas is by category. A *category* is a group of similar things. When you organize your ideas by category, writing is easier. You know which ideas to group together. Also, the reader can understand your writing better when similar ideas are grouped together.

Look at how Sara organized her ideas by category.

Adam

appearance	life	personality
curly, dark brown hair	younger brother	funny – plays jokes
brown eyes	10 years old	sweet – loves animals
a little heavy	the youngest	smart – loves school
short for his age	goes to school everyday	cheerful – talks and laughs a lot
missing a few teeth	plays soccer after school	
	follows my brother around	
	drives him crazy	

Answer these questions with a partner.

1 What three categories did Sara use to organize her information?

_____

_____

2 Sara did not use all of the words from her brainstorming list. Which words are not in her category list? Why were they left out?

_____

_____

3 She also added some new ideas. What are they?

_____

_____

Your turn ↶

Organize your brainstorming ideas into categories on your paper. Take out any irrelevant ideas. Then add more ideas if you want.

B Plan your writing

> ### TOPIC SENTENCE AND SUPPORTING SENTENCES
>
> In English, a paragraph is usually about one main idea. The *topic sentence* tells us the main idea. It is usually the first sentence in a paragraph.
>
> All of the other sentences in the paragraph are about the topic sentence. They must all be relevant to the main idea. These sentences are called *supporting sentences*. Supporting sentences help the reader understand the main idea by giving more information about it. Supporting sentences about similar ideas should be grouped together in the paragraph.

Practice 1

Read the first draft of Sara's paragraph about Adam. It has not been revised or edited yet. Then, answer the following questions with a partner.

1 What is the main idea of her paragraph?
2 Where does she tell you the main idea? Find the topic sentence of the paragraph.
3 What order of categories did Sara use? What category did she write about first, second, and third?

Adam

Adam is a delightful boy. My wonderful younger brother. He is ten years old and the youngest in our family. He has dark, curly hair. And big, brown eyes. He often smiles. Then you can see his big, wide smile. He short for his age and a little heavy. Adam goes to school every day he often plays soccer with his friends after school. They aren't very good, but they have a lot of fun. Also loves to follow my teenage brother around. He drives my brother crazy! Adam is a sweet boy, he really loves animals. Sometimes, he tries to take care of hurt wild animals. Also, very smart. He loves school, and he gets good grades. I love him because he is funny and cheerful, too. He talks and laughs a lot, he makes everyone laugh with him. Now, I in this country, and I miss him very much.

Practice 2

Each group of sentences has one topic sentence and three supporting sentences. Write a *T* next to the topic sentence and *S* next to the supporting sentences.

1 _____ **a** Amy always understands me.

_____ **b** Amy is special to me.

_____ **c** I think Amy is beautiful.

_____ **d** I love the wild way Amy dances.

2 _____ **a** To me, my father is a great man.

_____ **b** My father is an excellent lawyer.

_____ **c** My father loves his family.

_____ **d** My father always has time for me.

3 _____ **a** Chris likes to have a good time.

_____ **b** Chris is short and has wavy, brown hair.

_____ **c** Chris is one of my favorite people.

_____ **d** Every day, Chris runs several miles.

Practice 3

Read the paragraph below. Then, read the sentences that follow the paragraph. Check (✓) all the sentences that are good topic sentences for this paragraph.

My Grandmother

_____. She was born 77 years ago in England. When she was a baby, her family moved to the United States. After high school, she worked in a bakery until she married my grandfather. She can still make delicious cakes! My grandfather died five years ago, so she lives with us now. My grandmother is not patient, but she never gets angry with me. She always listens to me and helps me with my problems.

_____ **1** My grandmother is tall and thin.

_____ **2** I think my grandmother is a wonderful person.

_____ **3** An important person in my life is my grandmother.

_____ **4** My grandmother had five children.

_____ **5** Let me tell you about Grandma.

_____ **6** My grandmother can make me laugh when I am sad.

Practice 4

Read the student paragraph below. Then, read the sentences that follow the paragraph. Check (✓) all the sentences that are good topic sentences for this paragraph.

Capito

_____. He's a medium-size Labrador retriever with short, yellow hair and a long tail. In the house, he is always with me. When he comes to me, he hits everything with his tail. He also likes to come with me for a walk or a drive. Capito loves water. He loves to swim, play in the rain, and even play with the water in his bowl. He is a good student. He likes to learn, and he knows a lot of commands. Also, Capito is very gentle. He runs after cats, but he doesn't touch them.

_____ 1 Capito is my dog and my friend.

_____ 2 Capito's face is big and square.

_____ 3 My dog is seven years old.

_____ 4 Capito is my lovable dog.

_____ 5 Capito is my wonderful pet.

Practice 5

Write a topic sentence for this paragraph.

A Teacher to Remember

_____. He was a tall, thin man with red hair, and he wore thick glasses. In the classroom, he was always moving. He never sat still. When he was teaching, he always walked around, swung his arms, or tapped his feet. Mr. Jenkins put his energy into teaching us literature and drama at my high school. He was an excellent teacher. He taught us to love literature. Also, he helped the students present two school plays every year. Mr. Jenkins cared a lot about his students, too. He always had time to talk to students about their problems. I hope that I can be like him when I am a teacher.

C Write the first draft

Get comfortable, relax, and think about your important person. Use your list of categories to write a paragraph about that person. Remember, you will revise and edit your paragraph later, so don't worry about making mistakes.

III REVISING YOUR WRITING

A Analyze a paragraph

Read a student's first draft below. Then answer these questions. Talk about your answers with your class.

1 What do you like about this paragraph?
2 Is the paragraph about one main idea?
3 Is there a good topic sentence?
4 Are all of the supporting sentences relevant to the main idea?
5 Are the supporting sentences grouped in categories?

My Friend

Eun Hee and I met in high school. When I left Korea, she cried. Eun Hee works at General Hospital, and she is never absent from work. She likes to take care of the patients, but she doesn't like the doctors. She says they don't respect the nurses. One doctor always shouts at the nurses. On the weekends, she goes to the mountains or visits an interesting place. Eun Hee is very active. If there is something that she wants to do, she does it. She is cheerful and talkative. When I had a long face and was sad, she talked cheerfully to me. Eun Hee is tall and very thin. She has small, brown eyes and long, curly, dark brown hair. She looks like Olive Oyl in the Popeye cartoons. Olive Oyl is Popeye's girlfriend. Sometimes, when my friends and I were serious, she told jokes to us. I love her, and I want to see her again soon.

B Revise your writing

Exchange the first draft of your paragraph with a partner. Read your partner's paper, and answer these questions about it.

1 What do you like about your partner's paper? Put a star next to any ideas or sentences that you like.
2 Is there anything that you do not understand? Put a question mark (?) in the margin next to any sentence that you do not understand.

3 Is there a topic sentence about the main idea? If there is a topic sentence, underline it and write *TS* above it. If there is no topic sentence, write "no topic sentence" at the top of the page.

4 Do all of the supporting sentences give information about the topic sentence? Are there any irrelevant sentences? Put parentheses ( ) around any irrelevant sentences.

5 On the bottom of your partner's paper, write one question about the paragraph. Ask about something you want to know about the important person.

Your turn ✐

Get your paragraph back from your partner. Reread your paragraph. Then, follow these steps to revise it.

1 If there are any question marks on your paper, write those sentences more clearly. Ask your teacher or your partner for help if you need it.

2 Answer your partner's question about your important person. Add that information to your paper if you want to.

3 Think about the questions in *Analyze a paragraph* on page 29. Do you need to make any other changes to your own paper?

4 Look at your *Progress Check* on page 17 of Chapter 1. Use it to help you revise your paragraph.

C Write the second draft

Rewrite your paragraph, and make any changes that you need. Write a title at the top of your paragraph.

IV EDITING YOUR WRITING

A Focus on sentence grammar

> #### FRAGMENTS
>
> In English, every sentence must have both a subject and a verb. If a sentence does not have both a subject and a verb, it is called a fragment. *Fragment* means "broken piece." A sentence fragment is only a piece of a sentence, not a complete sentence.
>
> There are three problems a fragment can have.
>
> - No subject
>   Also loves to follow my teenage brother around.
>
> - No verb
>   He short for his age and a little heavy.
>
> - No subject or verb
>   And big, brown eyes.

Practice 6

Read each sentence fragment and identify the problem. Write *NS* for no subject, *NV* for no verb, or *NSV* for no subject or verb.

_____ **1** My wonderful old grandmother.

_____ **2** Every morning of her long life.

_____ **3** Fixes breakfast for her family.

_____ **4** A cigarette always in her mouth.

_____ **5** Often worry about her.

_____ **6** An important person in my family.

Practice 7

Write *F* next to the fragments and *S* next to the complete sentences.

_____ **1** My niece is a special person in my life.

_____ **2** Only nine months old.

_____ **3** Her silky, black hair.

_____ **4** Likes to play at three in the morning!

_____ **5** My niece is very cute.

_____ **6** I love her.

CORRECTING A FRAGMENT

There are several ways to correct a fragment.

- Add a subject or a verb.

  Fragment: Also loves to follow my teenage brother around.

  Sentence: He also loves to follow my teenage brother around.

  Fragment: He short for his age and a little heavy.

  Sentence: He is short for his age and a little heavy.

- Add a subject and a verb.

  Fragment: My wonderful little brother.

  Sentence: He is my wonderful little brother.

- Add the fragment to another sentence.

  Fragment: And big brown eyes.

  Sentence: He has dark, curly hair and big brown eyes.

Practice 8

Read the following pairs of sentences. In each pair, one sentence is a fragment. Correct the fragment either by adding something to it or by joining it to the other sentence. There are several possible ways to fix each fragment. Write only one.

1 An important person in my life is not a person. He a cat.
   He is a cat.

2 One night he came to my door. And cried for food.

3 After that first night. Tramp has stayed with me.

4 Tramp is a large, gray cat. With one torn ear.

5 He sleeps a lot during the day. And hunts at night.

6 He tries to catch mice. Too fast for him.

7 My cat and some of the neighborhood cats. They fight sometimes.

8 In the evenings. Tramp watches TV with me.

9 Likes to sleep on my bed. At night.

10 Day or night, he a good friend to me. He keeps me company.

RUN-ON SENTENCES

A common writing mistake is a run-on sentence. A run-on sentence happens when two simple sentences are run together without correct punctuation to separate them.

   Run-on sentences: Adam is a sweet boy he really loves animals.
                      Adam is a sweet boy, he really loves animals.

To correct a run-on sentence, make it into two simple sentences. Put a period at the end of the first subject and verb group. Start the second sentence with a capital letter.

   Correct sentences: Adam is a sweet boy. He really loves animals.

Practice 9

Write *RO* next to the run-on sentences and *CS* next to correct sentences.

_RO_ **1** I want to own a company some day I hope to be a good boss.

_____ **2** I remember my first boss, he was terrible.

_____ **3** He never listened to us. He only shouted.

_____ **4** He helped some workers a lot other workers got no help from him.

_____ **5** He also stole from the company and blamed the workers for it.

Practice 10

Correct these run-on sentences.

1 A person important to me is my twin sister her name is Jody.

_____

_____

2 Jody and I are the same height, we both have blonde hair and green eyes.

_____

_____

3 We enjoy the same things for example, we both love hot dogs and chess.

_____

_____

4 Jody understands me better than anyone, she knows me very well.

_____

_____

5 We live in different cities we usually visit each other on weekends.

_____

_____

6 I can't live without my twin, once a day we call each other and talk on the telephone.

_____

_____

Practice 11

In this paragraph, some of the sentences are run-ons. To correct the run-on sentences, add periods and capital letters. Take out commas if you need to.

Mac

¹Mac is a special guy. ^W/we have been friends for a long time. ²Now we are at college together. ³Mac is tall and very thin, my mother calls him Stringbean. ⁴He has a tough life. ⁵He takes classes during the day and drives a taxi every night. ⁶His father drinks too much and sometimes fights with his mother Mac tries to help her. ⁷He also likes to have a good time. ⁸On his night off, he goes out with his girlfriend, sometimes he drives to the beach at three in the morning! ⁹He is amazing.

Practice 12

Read Sara's paragraph about Adam. Underline all of the subjects and verbs. Then, find and correct the fragments and run-on sentences.

Adam

¹Adam is a delightful boy. ²My wonderful younger brother. ³He is ten years old and the youngest in our family. ⁴He has dark, curly hair. ⁵And big, brown eyes. ⁶He often smiles. ⁷Then you can see his big, wide smile. ⁸He short for his age and a little heavy. ⁹Adam goes to school every day he often plays soccer with his friends after school. ¹⁰They aren't very good, but they have a lot of fun. ¹¹Also loves to follow my teenage brother around. ¹²He drives my brother crazy! ¹³Adam is a sweet boy, he really loves animals. ¹⁴Sometimes, he tries to take care of hurt wild animals. ¹⁵Also, very smart. ¹⁶He loves school, and he gets good grades. ¹⁷I love him because he is funny and cheerful, too. ¹⁸He talks and laughs a lot, he makes everyone laugh with him. ¹⁹Now, I in this country, and I miss him very much.

B Edit your writing

Use the *Editing Checklist* below to edit your second draft. Follow these steps.

1 Underline all of the subjects in your sentences. Circle all of the verbs.

2 Using the checklist, look for only one kind of mistake each time you read your paragraph. For example, the first time you read your paragraph, ask yourself, "Does every sentence have a subject and a verb?" The next time you read it, look for a different kind of mistake.

3 Use *Quick Check* on pages 123–140 to help you fix your mistakes.

4 Look at your *Progress Check* on page 17 of Chapter 1. Use it to help you edit your paragraph.

EDITING CHECKLIST ✓

Look at each sentence.

☐ **1** Does every sentence have a subject and verb?

☐ **2** Are there any fragments?

☐ **3** Are there any run-on sentences?

Look at each verb.

☐ **4** Do all of the verbs agree with their subjects?

☐ **5** Are all of the verbs the correct tense?

☐ **6** Are all of the verbs the correct form?

Look at the punctuation and capitalization.

☐ **7** Does each sentence begin with a capital letter?

☐ **8** Does each sentence end with the correct punctuation?

Look at the words.

☐ **9** Is each word spelled correctly?

C Write the final draft

Write your final draft, including your changes and corrections. Use correct format.

A Share your writing

Exchange papers with a partner. Read and talk about your papers. Compare your important people. How are they the same or different? Ask any questions that you have about your partner's important person.

B Check your progress

After you get your paper back from your teacher, complete the *Progress Check* below.

PROGRESS CHECK

Date: _____

Paragraph title: _____

Things I did well in this paragraph:

_____

_____

_____

Things I need to work on in my next paragraph:

_____

_____

_____

Look at your *Progress Check* on page 17 of Chapter 1. How did you improve your writing in this paragraph?

_____

_____

_____

The Weekend

The weekend begins on Friday night and ends on Sunday night. Our weekend lives are usually different from our weekday lives. We may relax and have fun. We may also work at weekend jobs or study. The weekend is a time to clean the house, go shopping, and go to parties!

In this chapter, you will write a paragraph about your weekend.

A Picture this

Answer the questions about each photograph with your class or in a small group.

1 Where is this activity happening?
2 What is happening in the photograph?
3 Do you do activities like this on the weekend?

B Get ideas

AN IDEA WEB

You have used brainstorming as one way to get ideas. Another way to get ideas is by making an idea web. A spiderweb is made of connecting threads; an *idea web* is made of connecting ideas. As in brainstorming, the purpose of an idea web is to write down as many connected ideas as possible.

Here are the steps for making an idea web.

1 In the center of your paper, write a word or a phrase that gives the topic of the paragraph that you will write.

2 Draw a circle around your topic. Then, draw lines going away from the circle.

3 At the end of each line, write a word or phrase related to your topic.

4 Then, draw lines away from those words or phrases, and write other ideas related to them.

Look at this example of an idea web for the topic *Weekday*. Draw more lines and add your own ideas to the web. Then talk about this web with your class.

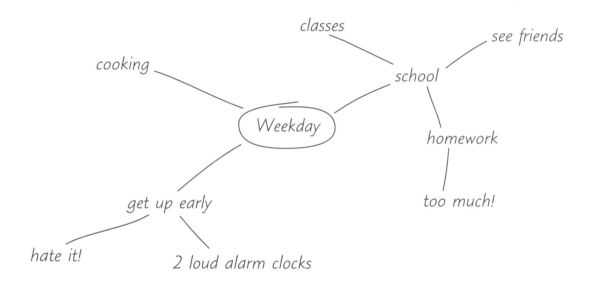

Your turn ↺

Choose one weekend day, either Saturday or Sunday, and make your own personal idea web for it on piece of paper. Follow the steps in the box above. Look at the photographs on the opposite page for ideas.

A Organize your ideas

Follow these steps to organize your ideas for your paragraph.

1 Look at your idea web, and circle the ideas you want to use. You can use all of them if you want.

2 Look at the ideas that you have circled. Many of them are probably about things that you do during that day. What do you do first? Put a number *1* next to it. What do you do second? Put a number *2* next to it. Continue to number all of the other circled ideas.

ORGANIZING BY TIME ORDER

There are many ways to organize your writing. When you organize your ideas by telling what happened first, second, third, and so on, you are organizing by *time order*. In this chapter, you will write about a day, so you will use time order to organize your paragraph.

B Plan your writing

Read these two drafts of a paragraph about Saturday. With your class, talk about which one is easier to understand and why.

Draft A

Saturday

Saturday is the worst day and the best day of the week for me. I usually wake up late. First, I take a shower, and then, I sometimes wash my car. After that, I eat lunch. I don't eat breakfast on Saturday because I get up late. After I eat lunch, I go to my uncle's store where I work. That is the start of a terrible time. It is very difficult to sell things because I cannot understand English. I am especially afraid of the telephone. I always make mistakes. While I am working in the store, I feel like I am walking in a hell. After work, I go back home. I eat dinner and then stay in my room to study or read. At about ten o'clock, I call my girlfriend in my country. It is the happiest time of the week. If I could not call her, I would go back to my country. After I call my girlfriend, I go to bed and sleep.

Draft B

Saturday

Saturday is the worst day and the best day of the week for me. I usually wake up late. I take a shower, and I sometimes wash my car. I eat lunch. I don't eat breakfast on Saturday because I get up late. I go to my uncle's store where I work. That is the start of a terrible time. It is very difficult to sell things because I cannot understand English. I am especially afraid of the telephone. I always make mistakes. While I am working in the store, I feel like I am walking in a hell. I go back home. I eat dinner and then stay in my room to study or read. I call my girlfriend in my country. It is the happiest time of the week. If I could not call her, I would go back to my country. I go to bed and sleep.

TRANSITIONS

When you write your paragraph, you need to use words to tell the reader what you do first, second, and so on. Most writers use words called transitions to tell the order that something happened in. *Transition* means "change," and we use transitions to show a time change in the paragraph.

These words and phrases are transitions.

first	in the morning
next	in the afternoon
then	in the evening
after that	at night
later	at ten o'clock
finally	at midnight

Notice that the transition usually comes at the beginning of a sentence and is followed by a comma.

<u>After that</u>, I eat lunch.
   transition

<u>At ten o'clock</u>, I call my girlfriend in my country.
   transition

Practice 1

Write the transitions in the paragraph below. Some sentences have several possible answers. Write only one. Be sure to use commas where you need them.

The Best Day of the Week

Sunday is my favorite day of the week. _____ (1) I sleep a long time. _____ (2) I get up and eat a huge breakfast. I read the newspaper while I eat. _____ (3) I do some chores. My apartment is small, so it is easy to clean. I take my dirty clothes to a laundromat. _____ (4) I call a friend, and we go shopping or to the gym. _____ (5) we pick up a pizza and go back to my place to eat it. _____ (6) we rent a video or watch a movie on TV. My friend goes home early because we both have classes on Monday. _____ (7) I listen to music and finish my homework in the quiet night.

C Write the first draft

Get comfortable, relax, and write the first draft of your paragraph. Use your idea web to tell what you do either on Saturday or on Sunday.

III REVISING YOUR WRITING

A Analyze a paragraph

Read a student's first draft on the next page. It has not been revised or edited yet. Then, answer these questions. Talk about your answers with your class.

1 What do you like about this paragraph?
2 Is the paragraph about one main idea?
3 Is there a good topic sentence?
4 Are all of the supporting sentences relevant to the main idea?
5 Are the supporting sentences organized in time order?
6 Did the writer use enough transitions?

My Sunday

This is about my Sunday. I usually wake up late, at one o'clock or two o'clock. Then, I take a shower before I eat lunch. But sometimes on Sunday morning, I wake up early. I play basketball with my friends at the university. We go to a grocery store to buy food and to the mall to buy clothes. My roommate buys a lot of clothes and CDs every week. I don't know why he does that. He doesn't need them. I always go to my aunt's house. My aunt, my cousins, and I eat lunch and talk to each other. In the afternoon, I usually go to a movie theater with my cousins. I go back to my dormitory. I do my homework and write in my journal in the evening. But first, I always talk on the phone to my family and friends. Then, my roommates and I listen to music and talk about the future in my dorm room. Finally, I organize my backpack before I go to bed. I always go to sleep early on Sunday night.

B Revise your writing

Exchange first drafts with a partner. Read your partner's paragraph, and answer these questions about it.

1 Which transitions did your partner use show the time order in the paragraph? Write them here.

____

____

2 Does your partner's paragraph need any more transitions? Put parentheses ( ) around any sentence that needs a transition.

Your turn

Get your paragraph back from your partner. Reread your paragraph, and answer these questions.

1 Do you need to add any transitions?
2 Ask yourself the questions in *Analyze a paragraph* on the opposite page. Do you need to make any changes?
3 Look at your *Progress Check* on page 36 of Chapter 2. Use it to help you revise your paragraph.

C Write the second draft

Rewrite your paragraph, and make any changes that you need. Write a title at the top of your paper.

A Focus on sentence grammar

Read a student's paragraph about her favorite weekend day, Saturday. Can you think of a way to make the sentences better? Discuss your ideas with your class.

Saturday

Saturday is my favorite day. I don't go to school. I get up late in the morning. First, I call my mother. We talk about my week. Next, I vacuum the apartment. My sister cooks us breakfast. I can cook. My sister is a better cook than I. After breakfast, I go shopping. I usually buy some clothes. In the afternoon, I meet my boyfriend. We go to interesting places such as the city, the beach near the bridge, and famous historic districts. I don't know my way around the city. He guides me. I like walking. We walk together and talk to each other. Later, we eat dinner at a restaurant. He takes me home. Sometimes we watch a video. Other times we watch an old movie on TV. Then, he goes home. I get ready for bed and talk to my sister about the day. I am usually very tired. I go to sleep quickly. Then, my night of dreams begins.

COMPOUND SENTENCES

All of the sentences in the paragraph "Saturday" are simple sentences. A simple sentence has a subject group and a verb group. Simple sentences are fine, but your paragraph might sound boring if all of your sentences are simple sentences. To solve this problem, you can join two simple sentences together to make a *compound sentence.*

I don't go to school. + I get up late in the morning.
   simple sentence   +   simple sentence

I don't go to school, so I get up late in the morning.
           compound sentence

Practice **2**

Write *S* next to the simple sentences. Write *C* next to the compound sentences.

_____ **1** My family likes to spend Sundays together.

_____ **2** I go out with my friends on Saturdays, but I stay home on Sundays.

_____ **3** My mother cooks a big meal, or we go out to eat at a restaurant.

_____ **4** Sometimes, my cousins come to visit us and eat with us.

_____ **5** I love our Sundays together, and I will always remember them.

COORDINATING CONJUNCTIONS

Two simple sentences can join together to form a compound sentence. When two sentences are joined in this way, the two sentences are called by a different name. They are called *independent clauses*, and the word that joins them is called a *coordinating conjunction*.

A compound sentence is made of two independent clauses joined by a coordinating conjunction.

I don't go to school, so I get up late in the morning.
independent clause   +   independent clause

A conjunction is a word that joins ideas. A coordinating conjunction joins ideas that are the same, or equal. The coordinating conjunctions that we use most often are *and, but, so,* and *or*. Notice that there is a comma before the coordinating conjunction.

- **And** shows added information.

    Rob and Sara go to the library, **and** they study for three hours.
    independent clause   CC   independent clause

- **But** shows something different or a contrast.

    I go to work on Saturday, **but** I don't work on Sunday.
    independent clause   CC   independent clause

- **So** shows the result of something

    Kim misses her family, **so** she calls them every weekend.
    independent clause   CC   independent clause

- **Or** shows two different choices

    In the afternoon, I clean my room, **or** I read a book.
    independent clause   CC   independent clause

Practice 3

These sentences are about Sunday activities. Match the beginning of each sentence with its ending. Write the letter in the blank.

_d_	**1** Tony works late on Saturday night,	**a**	and she drinks it on the balcony.
_____	**2** Samia takes her children to the park,	**b**	and they eat out after church.
_____	**3** Shu Fen relaxes in her room all day,	**c**	but on a rainy day, she watches TV.
_____	**4** Yoji and his girlfriend go to a movie,	**d**	so he sleeps late on Sunday.
_____	**5** In the morning, Lisa makes coffee,	**e**	or he plays tennis with a friend.
_____	**6** On a good day, Maria takes a walk,	**f**	but she studies at night.
_____	**7** Ji Yeon goes to church with her family,	**g**	so her children love Sunday.
_____	**8** After lunch, Ahmed works on his car,	**h**	or they rent a video.

Practice 4

Join each pair of simple sentences to make one compound sentence. Use a coordinating conjunction (*and, but, so, or*). Be sure to punctuate the sentence correctly.

1 I like to stay up late to watch old movies on TV. My husband likes to go to bed early.

_____

_____

2 Ken washes cars on Saturday. He works on Sunday, too.

_____

_____

3 Carol loves art. She goes to the museum every Saturday.

_____

_____

4 Christy and Ben go dancing Saturday night. They rent a video.

_____

_____

5 We clean our apartment on Saturday. It's messy again on Sunday.

_____

_____

Practice 5

Finish these compound sentences with your own words.

1 I like to sleep late, but _____

_____

2 We don't have school on the weekend, so _____

_____

3 I enjoy Sunday dinner with my family, or _____

_____

4 On Saturday afternoon, I call my best friend, and _____

_____

5 I don't have time to relax during the week, so _____

_____

Practice 6

This paragraph has no punctuation. Add periods and commas to make simple and compound sentences. Add capital letters as needed. The first one has been done for you.

My Saturdays

On Saturdays, I live an interesting life. I live by the ocean and I work there for a very old woman in the past she loved to stand on the beach and watch the sunrise but now she is too old to leave her house my job is to take pictures of the sunrise for her every Saturday morning first I leave my house in the dark and I walk to the beach with my camera then I take lots of pictures of the sunrise I am often sleepy but I love to be near the ocean in the morning next I go home and eat a big breakfast after that I print out the pictures from my computer in the afternoon I take the pictures to the old woman and we talk about the ocean she pays me so I have money to go out with my boyfriend at night we go to a baseball game or we have fun at an amusement park later we walk by the ocean in the moonlight my Saturday begins and ends by the ocean

---

Practice 7

Look at the following paragraph about Saturday again. With a partner, join some of the simple sentences to make compound sentences. Then, rewrite the paragraph on a separate piece of paper.

Saturday

Saturday is my favorite day. I don't go to school. I get up late in the morning. First, I call my mother. We talk about my week. Next, I vacuum the apartment. My sister cooks us breakfast. I can cook. My sister is a better cook than I. After breakfast, I go shopping. I usually buy some clothes. In the afternoon, I meet my boyfriend. We go to interesting places such as the city, the beach near the bridge, and famous historic districts. I don't know my way around the city. He guides me. I like walking. We walk together and talk to each other. Later, we eat dinner at a restaurant. He takes me home. Sometimes we watch a video. Other times we watch an old movie on TV. Then, he goes home. I get ready for bed and talk to my sister about the day. I am usually very tired. I go to sleep quickly. Then, my night of dreams begins.

Your turn 🗸

Now look at your own paragraph about the weekend. Did you write any compound sentences? Can you join any simple sentences to make compound sentences?

B Edit your writing

Use the *Editing Checklist* below to edit your paragraph. Follow these steps.

1 Underline all of the subjects in your sentences. Circle all of the verbs.
2 Using the checklist, look for only one kind of mistake each time you read your paragraph. For example, the first time you read your paragraph, ask yourself, "Does each sentence have a subject and a verb?" The next time you read it, look for a different kind of mistake.
3 Use *Quick Check* on pages 123–140 to help you fix your mistakes.
4 Look at your *Progress Check* on page 36 of Chapter 2. Use it to help you edit your paragraph.

EDITING CHECKLIST ☑

Look at each sentence.

☐ 1 Does every sentence have a subject and a verb?
☐ 2 Are there any fragments?
☐ 3 Are there any run-on sentences?

Look at each verb.

☐ 4 Do all of the verbs agree with their subjects?
☐ 5 Are all of the verbs the correct tense and form?

Look at the punctuation and capitalization.

☐ 6 Does each sentence begin with a capital letter?
☐ 7 Does each sentence end with the correct punctuation?
☐ 8 Is there a comma after each transition?
☐ 9 Is there a comma in each compound sentence?
☐ 10 Did you capitalize *Saturday* or *Sunday*?

Look at the words.

☐ 11 Is each word spelled correctly?

C Write the final draft

Write your final draft, including your changes and corrections. Use correct format.

A Share your writing

Follow these steps to share your writing in small groups.

1 Get into a small group. Read each paragraph in your group. On the back of the paper, write a sentence about the paragraph. Write about something you liked in the paragraph, or write about something that was interesting to you. Write only good things, and do not write about grammar. Sign your name.

2 When you get your paper back, read the comments on the back.

3 Ask each other any questions that you have.

B Check your progress

After you get your paragraph back from your teacher, complete the *Progress Check* below.

PROGRESS CHECK
Date: _____   Paragraph title: _____   Things I did well in this paragraph: _____   _____   _____   Things I need to work on in my next paragraph: _____   _____   _____   Look at your *Progress Check* on page 36 of Chapter 2. How did you improve your writing in this paragraph?   _____   _____   _____

A Scary or Funny Experience

Sometimes when friends and family are at a party, sitting around the dinner table, or just relaxing together, we tell stories. "I remember when . . . ," begins someone, and everyone ends up laughing. "I'll never forget . . . ," another person says, and everyone shivers with fear. All of us have stories from our own lives. Some stories are funny. Others are scary.

In this chapter, you will write either a funny or a scary story from your own life.

A Picture this

Answer the questions about each photograph with your class or in a small group.

1 What is happening in the photograph?
2 What do you think is going to happen next?
3 Did something like this happen to you?

B Get ideas

> ### TALKING TO GET IDEAS
>
> Talking with others is a good way to get ideas for your writing. When you tell a story, you try to make it interesting for the listeners. When you tell an interesting story, you can get many good ideas for writing that story.

Follow these steps to get ideas by telling your story.

1 Get in a small group with several other people.
2 Tell a true story from your own life. The story can be either a scary story or a funny story. It could be a memory from your childhood, about your family, about your friends, or about your time in school. It could be a ghost story that you have heard or a frightening experience from your own life.
3 As members of your group tell their stories, be sure to ask a lot of questions to help them think of ideas to include later in their own writing.

II PREPARING THE FIRST DRAFT

A Organize your ideas

To organize your ideas, make sure your story answers these six questions: *Who, What, When, Where, Why,* and *How.* Follow these steps to organize your ideas.

1 Find a partner whose story you have not heard.
2 Imagine that you are a newspaper reporter. Your assignment is to get information about your partner's scary or funny experience. Ask your partner the questions in the box below, and write down the answers on a piece of paper.
3 When you finish your interview, give your notes to your partner.
4 Read what your partner wrote. Is everything accurate? Do you need to add anything?

Interview questions

1 Was this a scary experience or a funny experience?
2 Who was there?
3 When did it happen?
4 Where did it happen?
5 What happened? Give a summary.
6 Why did it happen?
7 How did you and the others feel?

B Plan your writing

Practice 1

Read this student's paragraph. It is an interesting story, but it leaves the reader with many questions. After you read the paragraph, write some questions that you have about it on a separate piece of paper.

Draft A

A Scary and Funny Experience

I remember a time that was funny for me but scary for my sister. My sister was in her bedroom trying to sleep. I decided to make some strange noises and pretend to be a spirit or ghost. She couldn't sleep, so she called my mother. When my mother came, I stopped. My mother said, "I don't hear anything except the wind outside," and she went downstairs. I started again. My sister talked to herself and to the noises. After that, she called my mother again. My mother shouted at the spirits, too, and then she went downstairs again. Later, I couldn't keep quiet anymore, so I laughed. Then, my sister understood that I had made the noises.

Practice 2

Read Draft B of the paragraph. Answer the questions that follow with a partner.

Draft B

A Scary and Funny Experience

I remember a time that was funny for me but scary for my sister. It was about seven years ago, on a very dark night without a moon and with a lot of wind. My younger sister was in her bedroom trying to sleep. I decided to go to the attic over her room and make some strange noises. I pretended to be a spirit or ghost. I made scary sounds, banged on the floor, and howled like a dog. My sister couldn't sleep, and I could hear her moving around in her room. Finally, she called my mother. When my mother came, I stopped. My mother listened. Then, she said, "I don't hear anything except the wind outside," and she returned downstairs to watch TV. After a few minutes, I started again. My sister was very nervous. She talked to herself, and she told the ghost or animal or maybe spirits to go away. It was very funny, so it was very difficult for me not to laugh. After that, she called my mother again. This time, my mother came with a long stick. She shouted at the spirits so that my sister wouldn't worry. But my mother didn't believe in the spirits and soon returned to the TV.

After about an hour and a half, I couldn't keep quiet anymore. It was too funny. I started to laugh, and then my sister understood that I had made the noises. She was very angry. She shouted at me to come down from the attic. When I did, she said, "I can't sleep now because of you. You have to stay up all night with me." The next morning, my mother found us together. We were sitting on the floor back to back, and we were sleeping.

1 Were the questions you wrote in *Practice 1* answered in Draft B?
2 Which paragraph did you enjoy reading more, Draft A or B? Why?

DETAILS

Interesting stories have many details. *Details* are specific pieces of information that help us to understand a general idea better. When we write a story, details help the readers see the story in their minds.

Details tell us different kinds of information.

- **Facts:** information about who, what, when, where, why, and how
  It was about seven years ago, on a very dark night without a moon and with a lot of wind.

- **Senses:** information about what you see, hear, smell, touch, and taste
  My sister couldn't sleep, and I could hear her moving around in her room.

- **Emotions:** information about how the writer and the people in the story feel
  My sister was very nervous.

Practice **3**

Look at Draft B on the opposite page. Underline details that were added to give a clearer picture of the story. What kinds of information do the details give us?

Your turn ↻

Follow these steps to add details and plan your story.

1 Look again at the interview information your partner wrote in *Organize your ideas* on page 53. Can you add more details of fact, sense, or emotion? Add more details to make your story clearer and more interesting.

2 Reread the information on your interview page. Think about the best way to use the information to tell your story. You can number your ideas to help you put them in time order.

C Write the first draft

Write a paragraph telling your funny or scary story. Use your notes from the interview to help you write.

A Analyze a paragraph

Read a student's first draft below, and answer the questions. Then, talk about your answers with your class.

1 What do you like about this paragraph?
2 Is the paragraph about one main idea?
3 Is there a good topic sentence?
4 Are all of the supporting sentences relevant to the main idea?
5 Are the supporting sentences in good time order?
6 Underline any transitions. Did the writer use enough transitions?
7 Did the writer give three different kinds of details: facts, senses, and emotions?

A Scary Story

I remember about ten years ago when I stayed with some friends in my country. We were next to an old, empty house. We were talking about ghosts. Suddenly, someone said to me, "If you can go inside that house, I will give you 300 dollars." I thought about it. He gave me 300 dollars, and I went into the house. After I went inside the house, I was very scared because I had heard about this house. I was looking to the left and to the right because I don't like looking at anything scary. I got out of the house. I said, "Thank you, my God! I'm safe!" I didn't like that adventure, but I needed the money.

B Revise your writing

To help each other, you will read each other's scary and funny experiences. Enjoy the stories, and think about other details that you would like to know. Work in small groups, and follow these steps.

1 Collect all the papers from your group, and exchange them with another group.

2 Each person in your group will read all of the papers. For each paper, do the following:
   - Put a star next to one word, sentence, or detail that you like.
   - If you do not understand a sentence, put a question mark (?) next to it.
   - At the bottom of the paper, write one question about the story. Ask for more details about something in the paragraph.

Your turn

When you get your paragraph back, reread it. Then, answer these questions.

1 Are there any question marks on it? If so, rewrite those sentences more clearly.
2 Answer the questions on the bottom of your paper. Can you add details to make your story better?
3 Look back at your interview notes. Did you include everything that you wanted to include in your story?
4 Ask yourself the questions in *Analyze a paragraph* on the opposite page. Do you need to make any changes?
5 Look at your *Progress Check* on page 49 of Chapter 3. Use it to help you revise your paragraph.

C Write the second draft

Rewrite your paragraph, and make any changes that you need. Write a title at the top of your paper.

IV EDITING YOUR WRITING

A Focus on sentence grammar

> ### COMPOUND SENTENCES
>
> A *compound sentence* is made up of two simple sentences. In a compound sentence, the simple sentences are called independent clauses. There are usually only two independent clauses in one compound sentence. The clauses are joined by a coordinating conjunction (*and, or, but, so*). A comma is placed after the first independent clause.
>
> He gave me 300 dollars, **and** I went into the house.
> independent clause   CC   independent clause

Practice 4

Do these sentences fit the description of a compound sentence? With your class, talk about why or why not.

1 People have always talked about ghosts, and many books have been written about them, but people cannot agree on their existence.
2 Some people believe in ghosts others laugh at the idea, other people just aren't sure.
3 One student saw a ghost, and he'll never forget the experience he believes in them now.

RUN-ON SENTENCES

A common writing mistake is the compound run-on sentence. A compound sentence does not usually have more than two independent clauses. If it does, it is probably a compound *run-on sentence*. There are several types of mistakes that can result in compound run-on sentences.

- More than two independent clauses joined by coordinating conjunctions

  People have always talked about ghosts, and many books have been written about them, but people cannot agree on their existence.

- More than two independent clauses not joined by coordinating conjunctions

  Some people believe in ghosts others laugh at the idea, other people just aren't sure.

- A mix of the two kinds of run-on sentences

  One student saw a ghost, and he'll never forget the experience he believes in them now.

Practice 5

Read this student's story. Decide which sentences are run-ons. Write *RO* above the run-on sentences. Then, talk about your answers with your class.

A Visit

¹One night in my country, I couldn't sleep. ²I was alone in my bedroom, and my brother and sister were sleeping in their rooms. ³Outside, the weather was not good. ⁴It was raining hard my room was dark, and it was about three o'clock in the morning. ⁵I prayed to God, and I wished for sleep. ⁶Suddenly, I saw a young woman with long black hair in front of me, and soft light was coming from her, so I could see her clearly. ⁷She gave me a smile, but she was floating above the floor. ⁸I was scared at the sight, I couldn't do anything, then, she started to laugh. ⁹I turned the light on with a big effort, but she disappeared in front of me I went to the living room and sat there until morning. ¹⁰Even today, I can't forget that experience, and I hope she will never bother me again.

CORRECTING A RUN-ON SENTENCE

A run-on sentence is two or more independent clauses incorrectly joined together. To correct a run-on sentence, separate it into two or more good sentences. Follow these steps to correct a run-on sentence.

1 Find all of the independent clauses and coordinating conjunctions in the run-on.

2 Decide where to put in one or more periods to make several sentences.

3 Add or take out coordinating conjunctions where you need to.

4 Change the order of the clauses, if necessary.

There is usually more than one way to correct a run-on sentence. You can decide which way you like best.

Run-on sentence 1:

> People have always talked about ghosts, and many books have been written about them, but people cannot agree on their existence.

Correction 1:

> People have always talked about ghosts, and many books have been written about them. [...] gree on their existence.

> [...] talked about ghosts. Many books have been written about them, but [...] on their existence.

> [...] in ghosts others laugh at the idea, other people just aren't sure.

> [...] in ghosts, but others laugh at the idea. Other people just aren't sure.

> [...] in ghosts. Others laugh at the idea. Other people just aren't sure.

> [...] ghost, and he'll never forget the experience he believes in them now.

> [...] ghost, and he'll never forget the experience. He believes in them now.

> [...] ghost, so he believes in them now. He'll never forget the experience.

Practice 6

On a separate piece of paper, rewrite the paragraph "A Visit" in *Practice 5* on the opposite page. Correct the run-on sentences.

Practice 7

This student's paragraph has both simple and compound sentences, but there are many run-on sentences in it. Correct the run-on sentences by adding periods and capital letters. You will need to add or remove some commas. You might choose to add some coordinating conjunctions.

A Funny Story

¹A funny thing happened to my family three years ago. ²One evening, my parents, my brother, and I went to see a movie. ³After that, we went to eat dinner at a restaurant, we took a long time there, so we came back home about twelve o'clock. ⁴I opened the front door, I was very surprised. ⁵Somebody had scattered everything in my house. ⁶Books and records were on the floor, and the sofa was torn up. ⁷At that time, I heard a strange noise from my room, and I was sure that there was somebody in my room, and I wanted to be a hero, so I told my family, "Please, watch out. I will check my room." ⁸I walked slowly and quietly to my room and opened my door carefully. ⁹Suddenly, something jumped out the window it was a wild cat. ¹⁰We realized that the cat had scattered everything in our house. ¹¹I had forgotten to close the window. ¹²Then, we all laughed together.

Practice 8

This student's paragraph has both simple and compound sentences, but there are many run-on sentences in it. Correct the run-on sentences by adding periods and capital letters. You will need to add or remove some commas, and you might choose to add some coordinating conjunctions.

The student wrote about a terrible experience that happened in Texas. In 1987, a girl named Jessica fell down a well. Her rescuers had to drill a hole next to the well to reach her. The student imagined that she was Jessica and wrote the story from Jessica's point of view.

Jessica's Terrible Experience

¹When I was only 18 months old, something terrible happened to me. ²One day, I was playing outside with some other children, I fell into a well, a deep well. ³At first, I didn't know what happened, I asked myself, "Why is it so dark? Where is my mommy?" ⁴After a few minutes, I heard my mom call me, "Jessica, Jessica, where are you?" ⁵Her voice sounded very worried then, I knew I was in the well. ⁶I began to feel pain because my body had hit on the rocky sides of

the well. **7**I cried and called my mom, then I fell asleep.

    8After a long time, I woke up, I was still in the well, I started to hear a loud noise. **9**I didn't know what it was, but I thought maybe it was Superman. **10**He was coming to save my life. **11**I remembered in the cartoons, Superman always saves people's lives. **12**When I thought about that, I wasn't scared anymore. **13**I even felt a little happy because I would see Superman. **14**Finally, I saw him, but he forgot to wear his Superman clothes he forgot to wear his red cape. **15**However, I believe he was my Superman. **16**He took me up to see my mommy and daddy and they were both crying, and I cried, too. **17**I was rescued!

B Edit your writing

Use the *Editing Checklist* to edit your paragraph. Follow these steps.

1 Underline all of the subjects in your sentences. Circle all of the verbs.
2 Using the checklist, look for only one kind of mistake at a time.
3 Use *Quick Check* on pages 123–140 to help you fix your mistakes.
4 Look at your *Progress Check* on page 49 of Chapter 3. Use it to help you edit your paragraph.

EDITING CHECKLIST ☑

Look at each sentence.

☐ **1** Does every sentence have a subject and a verb?

☐ **2** Are there any run-on sentences?

☐ **3** Are there any fragments?

Look at each verb.

☐ **4** Do all of the verbs agree with their subjects?

☐ **5** Are all of the verbs the correct tense and form?

Look at the punctuation and capitalization.

☐ **6** Does each sentence begin with a capital letter?

☐ **7** Does each sentence end with the correct punctuation?

☐ **8** Is there a comma after each transition?

☐ **9** Is there a comma in each compound sentence?

Look at the words.

☐ **10** Is each word spelled correctly?

C Write the final draft

Write your final draft, including your changes and corrections. Use correct format.

V FOLLOWING UP

A Share your writing

Follow these steps to read your classmates' stories in small groups.

1 Get in a small group. Collect all of the paragraphs from your group, and exchange them for the paragraphs of another group.
2 Each person in the group will read all of the papers. Then, the group will decide which story is the most enjoyable to read.
3 The teacher will read each group's favorite story. The group will explain why they chose that story.

B Check your progress

After you get your paragraph back from your teacher, complete the *Progress Check* below.

PROGRESS CHECK

Date: _____

Paragraph title: _____

Things I did well in this paragraph:

_____

_____

_____

Things I need to work on in my next paragraph:

_____

_____

_____

Look at your *Progress Check* on page 49 of Chapter 3. How did you improve your writing in this paragraph?

_____

_____

_____

Holidays

Holidays! They are different from all other days of the year. When we hear the word *holiday,* we think of special food, clothes, and activities. We can close our eyes and remember certain sights, smells, sounds, and tastes. Most of all, we remember good times with our family and friends.

In this chapter, you will write about your favorite holiday.

A Picture this

Answer the questions about each photograph with your class or in a small group.

1 What is the name of the holiday?
2 What is happening in the photograph?
3 Do you celebrate the same holiday or a similar one?

B Get ideas

What is your favorite holiday? On a blank piece of paper, write the name of the holiday in the middle of the page. Draw a circle around it and make an idea web, as you did in Chapter 3 on page 39. Include in your web what you do on that holiday and also the sights, sounds, smells, and tastes.

A Organize your ideas

To organize the information from your web, fill out the chart below. Use the words and phrases from your web, and add more details.

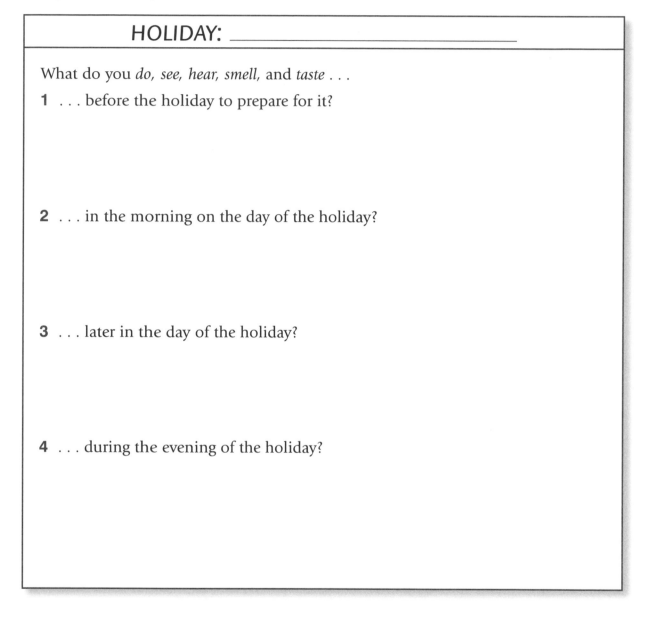

HOLIDAY: _____

What do you *do, see, hear, smell,* and *taste* . . .

1 . . . before the holiday to prepare for it?

2 . . . in the morning on the day of the holiday?

3 . . . later in the day of the holiday?

4 . . . during the evening of the holiday?

Your turn ↵

In a small group, talk about your chart. Follow these steps.

1 Using your chart, talk to other students about your favorite holiday.

2 Answer their questions, and write any more information on your chart.

3 Listen to the other students, and ask them questions about their holidays.

B Plan your writing

THE CONCLUSION

In English, a paragraph has three parts: a beginning, a middle, and an end. So far we have studied the beginning and the middle. The beginning tells the reader the main idea. Do you remember what that beginning sentence is called? The middle of a paragraph gives more information about the main idea. What do we call those sentences?

The end of a paragraph is called the *conclusion*. It is usually the last sentence of the paragraph. The conclusion is not just another supporting sentence. It has a separate job to do. The conclusion can do several things.

- It can remind the reader of the main idea. To do this, it repeats the topic sentence in different words.
- It can tell the writer's feelings or opinion about the ideas in the paragraph.
- It can do both of those things.

Practice 1

Read the paragraph below, and pay particular attention to the conclusion. Then answer the questions.

Eid al-Fitr

My favorite holiday of the year is Eid al-Fitr. It is the most famous holiday of the Muslim religion, and it comes after Ramadan. At the end of Ramadan before Eid, people prepare for the holiday. They go to the market to buy some new clothes and some sweets to eat. Mothers and daughters also clean the house. On the morning of Eid al-Fitr, people go to the mosque to pray. After that, families eat a huge breakfast together. Children get money from the older people to buy toys. In the afternoon, people go to visit each other to wish each other a happy Eid. Families also go out to eat in restaurants. Then, they go and have a good time in the park. In the evening, people celebrate together until midnight. Finally, they go to sleep because they have woken up early on that day. Eid al-Fitr is the best day of the year for me.

---

1 What is the conclusion of this paragraph?
2 Does it remind the reader of the main idea, tell the writer's feelings or opinion about Eid al-Fitr, or do both of those things?

Practice 2

Read the paragraph below. Then, answer the questions about the conclusion.

Chusok

Chusok is the most famous holiday in Korea. My family prepares many things the day before Chusok. First, we always make "songpyon." It is a traditional rice cake. After that, we clean our house. At the end of the day, we go to bed early because we have to get up early the next day. On this holiday morning, we all eat special food together. In the afternoon, we usually visit my father's sister. We spend the rest of the day at her home. We talk and play traditional games such as "yut." Finally, we go home to bed. I always feel happy and peaceful at the end of the day on Chusok.

---

1 What is the conclusion of this paragraph?

2 Does it remind the reader of the main idea, tell the writer's feelings or opinion about Chusok, or do both of those things?

Practice 3

Read this student's paragraph. Then, choose a good conclusion for it from the list below. There are several good conclusions. Put a check (✓) next to each good conclusion.

Happy New Year

I like the New Year in Japan because it is very exciting. On the night of December 31, my friends and I go to a karaoke bar. We are very loud and rowdy there. Just before midnight, we go to the temple because Japanese people pray for the new year. After 12 A.M., everyone says, "Akemashite. Omedetou gozaimasu." That means "Happy New Year." Then, we go to the beach to watch the sunrise. It is very, very beautiful. After that, we go home and eat delicious food together. In the afternoon, my family goes to my grandfather's house. We say, "Happy New Year" to all our relatives. When the children wish the adults a happy new year, the adults give them money. In the evening, we play card games for money. It's a lot of fun, but I sometimes lose. At midnight, we all go home.

_____ **1** I am exhausted, but very happy.

_____ **2** My grandmother has to clean up their house.

_____ **3** I take a bath before I go to bed.

_____ **4** I think that the New Year is the most wonderful time of the year.

_____ **5** During the year, I always smile when I remember our New Year fun.

_____ **6** The next morning, I hate to get up.

C Write the first draft

Use the information in your chart on page 65 to write a paragraph about your favorite holiday. Pay close attention to the purpose of your conclusion.

III REVISING YOUR WRITING

A Analyze a paragraph

Read a student's first draft below, and answer the questions. Then, talk about your answers with your class.

1 What do you like about this paragraph?
2 Is the paragraph about one main idea?
3 Is there a good topic sentence?
4 Are all of the supporting sentences relevant to the main idea?
5 Are the supporting sentences in a good order?
6 Circle the transitions in the paragraph. Did the writer use enough transitions?
7 Underline specific details. Did the writer give enough details?
8 Does the paragraph have a good conclusion?

Christmas

Before the holiday, when December is beginning, we start decorating the house. We put wreaths on the walls and other little decorations everywhere. We buy a pine tree, too. We put it in a corner of the living room, and we decorate it. This day has two meanings. The first meaning is the children's story of Father Christmas. Father Christmas comes in all the houses on the night of December 24 to give a present to good children. The second meaning is the religious meaning. It's the birthday of Jesus. On the morning of the holiday, I get up late and eat breakfast. After that, I finish wrapping presents. When I finish, I help my family with the last preparations for the day. In the evening, it starts. While our family and friends start to arrive, we have a little food and drink and talk with each other. Later, we go to eat a big dinner with one or two turkeys and lots of good food. Just before the dessert, an adult leaves the table and puts the presents under the Christmas tree. Then the adult calls to the children to hurry and see Father Christmas. When the children run into the room, the adults say, "Too late. He left quickly. He was in a hurry." The children are a little angry, but when they see the presents, they forget. Then everybody opens their presents. When everyone is finished, we go back to the table for my grandmother's special dessert. After dessert, the children play with their new toys, but the adults sit at the table for a long time. We drink and talk together until it is very late.

B Revise your writing

Follow these steps to revise your first draft.

1 Look at your own paper, and ask yourself the questions in *Analyze a paragraph* on the opposite page. What changes do you need to make?

2 Does your paragraph have a conclusion? If not, write several conclusions. Then, choose the best one to use at the end of your paragraph.

3 What does your conclusion do? Does it remind the reader of the main idea, give your feelings or opinion about your holiday, or do both of those things? Can you improve it? If your conclusion does not do any of those things, rewrite it.

4 Look at your *Progress Check* on page 62 of Chapter 4. Use it to help you revise your paragraph.

C Write the second draft

Rewrite your paragraph, and make any changes that you need. Write a title at the top of your paper.

IV EDITING YOUR WRITING

A Focus on sentence grammar

Practice 4

Look at these sentences. Write *S* next to the simple sentences. Write *C* next to the compound sentences, and circle the coordinating conjunction (*and, but, so, or*). Write *D* next to the ones that are a different kind of sentence (neither simple nor compound).

_____ 1 Independence Day is July 4 in the United States, so it is a national holiday.

_____ 2 My family and I spend the day at a lake near our house.

_____ 3 My younger sisters like to wear red, white, and blue clothes because those are the colors of the U.S. flag.

_____ 4 We also put an American flag on the picnic table.

_____ 5 After we eat lunch, my father rents a motorboat.

_____ 6 My youngest sister always begs to drive it, but he never lets her.

_____ 7 I always try waterskiing although I'm not very good at it.

_____ 8 We have a cookout with watermelon for dessert, and my sisters have fun spitting the seeds at each other.

_____ 9 When the day is over, we drive back to town to watch the fireworks.

_____ 10 The fireworks are beautiful, but they are over too soon.

COMPLEX SENTENCES

A *complex sentence* has two or more clauses in it. The sentences that are different in *Practice 4* on page 69 are complex sentences. They are neither simple nor compound. A compound sentence is made of two independent clauses. On the other hand, a complex sentence is made of one independent clause and one or more dependent clauses. A dependent clause cannot stand by itself as a sentence. It must always be joined to an independent clause.

<u>After we eat lunch</u> + my father rents a motorboat.
dependent clause   independent clause

I always try to water-ski + <u>although I'm not very good at it.</u>
independent clause   dependent clause

Notice that the dependent clause can come either before or after the independent clause. If the dependent clause is first, put a comma after it.

SUBORDINATING CONJUNCTIONS

How can you identify a dependent clause? A dependent clause begins with a *subordinating conjunction*. There are many subordinating conjunctions, but here are the most useful ones.

After – at a later time

 After we eat lunch, my father rents a motorboat.

Although – but

 My youngest sister always begs to drive the boat *although my father never lets her*.

Because – tells why

 My younger sisters like to wear red, white, and blue clothes *because those are the colors of the U.S. flag*.

Before – at an earlier time

 Before the sun sets, we find a high hill for watching the fireworks.

If – tells a possible situation

 If it rains on July 4, we are all disappointed.

Since – tells why, similar to *because*

 My younger sisters like to wear red, white, and blue clothes *since those are the colors of the U.S. flag*.

When – at that time

 When the day is over, we drive back to town to watch the fireworks.

While – happening at the same time as the independent clause

 While my sisters and I sunbathe, we watch the boys on the beach.

Your turn ✍

Underline the dependent clauses in the complex sentences you marked *D* in *Focus on sentence grammar* on page 69. Circle the subordinating conjunctions.

Practice 5

With a partner, match the clauses in the column on the left with the correct clauses in the column on the right. When you have matched all the clauses, you will have a complete story about a trick that was played on April Fool's Day.

An April Fool's Day Trick

"Fox" is both a wild animal and a common family name.

____c____ 1 Before Jim arrived at work,　　**a** since he wasn't busy.

_____ 2 Jim saw the message　　**b** he laughed at the joke.

_____ 3 Please call Mr. Fox　　**c** a coworker left a message on his desk.

_____ 4 If you don't know his number,　　**d** because Jim's coworker had left the number for the zoo.

_____ 5 Jim called the number right away　　**e** after you get in.

_____ 6 When someone answered the phone,　　**f** while he was looking through his mail.

_____ 7 The person on the phone laughed　　**g** Jim asked to speak to Mr. Fox.

_____ 8 Although Jim felt a little foolish,　　**h** it is 555-8720.

Practice 6

Read this student paragraph, and circle the correct subordinating conjunctions.

My Birthday

I think my birthday is the best "holiday" for me. Before / While my birthday
(1)
comes, I usually call my friends and tell them about my birthday. I joke and say
to them the most important thing is to prepare a present although / because it
(2)
is very important to me. In the morning on my birthday, I eat brown-seaweed
soup. Koreans always eat brown-seaweed soup after / when it is their birthday.
(3)
In the afternoon, I meet my friends, and we spend time together. After / If we
(4)
go bowling and play pool, we go to a club in the evening. My friends bring
a cake and light the candles. Since / When I blow them out, they push my
(5)
head into the cake. Then, we eat the cake, and it tastes wonderful. At night, the
terrible birthday ceremony starts. When / Because we go outside, my friends
(6)
make a circle. While / Before I stand in the center of the circle, they throw eggs
(7)
at me. The smell is incredible, but it isn't finished yet. They sprinkle flour on me.
Then, they give me presents. Although / After the smell is terrible, the presents
(8)
change my feelings. Anyway, I love my birthday if / since my friends and I have
(9)
a very good time on that day.

Practice 7

Read the following paragraph, and fill in each blank with a subordinating
conjunction that makes sense in that sentence. Some blanks may have more than one
possible answer. Capitalize as needed.

after	if	because	when
although	since	before	while

Summer Vacation

I think I am a typical student. _____ I like school, I *love*
(1)
vacations. _____ I am bored in school, I like to daydream about
(2)
my vacation plans. _____ summer vacation is coming, I feel the
(3)
happiest _____ it is the longest vacation. _____ final
(4)   (5)
exams are finished, I totally relax. I sleep late, eat at any time, and hang out

---

with my friends. Sometimes I have a part-time job _____ I am on
(6)
vacation. _____ I have a job, I have extra cash to have fun with.
(7)
Also, I go to the beach for a week _____ my parents rent a cottage
(8)
there. _____ my vacation is over, I always visit my grandparents.
(9)
I love to visit them _____ they let me do whatever I like. Finally,
(10)
summer ends, and it's back to school I go.

PUNCTUATING COMPLEX SENTENCES

If the dependent clause is at the beginning of the sentence, put a comma after the
dependent clause.

    If it rains on July 4, we are all disappointed.
        dependent clause

If the dependent clause is after the independent clause, do *not* put a comma after
the independent clause.

    We are all disappointed if it rains on July 4.
                        dependent clause

Practice 8

Punctuate this paragraph.

Halloween

¹Halloween is on October 31 when the weather is cool and crisp. ²Before
the day comes children and many adults prepare costumes. ³Although stores
sell them the best ones are homemade. ⁴Children wear their costumes to go
trick-or-treating in their neighborhoods after it gets dark. ⁵When they knock on
their neighbors' doors the children shout, "Trick or treat!" ⁶Then, the people in
the houses give them candy because the children will play tricks on them if they
don't give them anything. ⁷Although teenagers usually don't go trick-or-treating
they still love to play tricks on people. ⁸Adults often go to Halloween parties at
night because they enjoy dressing in costumes and acting like children. ⁹Parents
also enjoy eating their children's Halloween candy after the children are in bed!
¹⁰When Halloween comes children of all ages are happy.

Practice 9

Join each pair of sentences to make one complex sentence. Use a subordinating conjunction in each sentence, and punctuate the sentences correctly.

Halloween Revenge

1 Jason and Joe don't like their next door neighbor. He complains about their loud music.

_____

_____

2 Halloween came. They decided to play a trick on him.

_____

_____

3 Jason kept watch. Joe put toilet paper all over their neighbor's trees and bushes.

_____

_____

4 They hid behind some bushes. They finished.

_____

_____

5 The neighbor opened the door for some children. Jason and Joe were delighted to see the surprise on his face.

_____

_____

6 The neighbor went to work the next morning. He had to clean up the mess.

_____

_____

7 The neighbor asked lots of people. He never knew who did it.

_____

_____

Your turn ↩

Study the sentences in your paragraph. Do you have any complex sentences? If you do, underline the subordinating conjunctions. Can you join together any other sentences to make a complex sentence?

B Edit your writing

Use the *Editing Checklist* to edit your paragraph for run-on sentences and other problems. Follow these steps.

1 Underline all of the subjects in your sentences. Circle all of the verbs.

2 Using the checklist, look for only one kind of mistake at a time.

3 Use *Quick Check* on pages 123–140 to help you fix your mistakes.

4 Look at your *Progress Check* on page 62 of Chapter 4. Use it to help you edit your paragraph.

EDITING CHECKLIST ☑

Look at each sentence.

☐ **1** Does every sentence have a subject and a verb?

☐ **2** Are there any fragments?

☐ **3** Are there any run-on sentences?

Look at each verb.

☐ **4** Do all of the verbs agree with their subjects?

☐ **5** Are all of the verbs the correct tense and form?

Look at the punctuation and capitalization.

☐ **6** Does each sentence begin with a capital letter?

☐ **7** Does each sentence end with the correct punctuation?

☐ **8** Is there a comma in each compound sentence?

☐ **9** Are there commas where they are needed in complex sentences?

☐ **10** Did you capitalize the name of the holiday?

Look at the words.

☐ **11** Is each word spelled correctly?

C Write the final draft

Write your final draft, including your changes and corrections. Use correct format.

A Share your writing

Exchange papers with a partner, and read about how your partner celebrates his or her chosen holiday. If possible, exchange papers with someone who wrote about the same holiday that you did. Talk about your papers.

B Check your progress

After you get your paper back from your teacher, complete the *Progress Check* below.

PROGRESS CHECK

Date: _____

Paragraph title: _____

Things I did well in this paragraph:

_____

_____

_____

Things I need to work on in my next paragraph:

_____

_____

_____

Look at your *Progress Check* on page 62 of Chapter 4. How did you improve your writing in this paragraph?

_____

_____

_____

Telling Stories

Some people write books while other people write movies, songs, or TV shows. Although not everyone can do those things, most of us can make up stories. Did you ever make up a funny story to make your friends laugh? Did you ever make up a story to tell a child at bedtime?

In this chapter, you will use your imagination to write the ending to a story.

A Picture this

Answer the questions about each photograph with your class or in a small group.

1 Who is telling a story?
2 What kind of story is the person telling?
3 Why is the person telling a story?

B Get ideas

Read the beginnings of the following three stories. After you finish reading, follow these steps.

1 Decide which story you would like to finish.
2 Get in a group with other students who want to finish the same story.
3 Talk about possible endings for the story. Write down ideas and helpful vocabulary as you talk. Keep in mind, however, that you will write your own story, not one group story. Your ending should be different from other students' endings.

Story 1

One Dark Night

"Good night! It was a great party!" I waved to my friend who was standing at the front door, and I started walking down the road to my house. I live a little way out of town, but I had often walked home from my friend's house.

It was dark, very dark. There was no moon in the sky. It was a little chilly too, and soon, to my dismay, it started to rain. As I walked, a strong wind blew buckets of rain into my face. I was cold, wet, and miserable.

"If only I could find a place to wait until the rain stops," I thought. Luckily, in a few minutes, I saw a place. It was a small, old garage, and its door was banging open in the wind. I stepped inside, out of the wind and rain, and immediately felt better. I wasn't happy for long, though, because something – or was it someone – was in the garage with me.

Story 2

Mystery in the Dark

Laura closed her book, stood up, and stretched. It was ten o'clock, and she had been studying in the library for three hours. It was time to go to the dorm and relax. While she walked across the dark college campus to her dormitory, she thought about a hot bath and some good music.

When she arrived at her floor of the dorm, everything was quiet. No one was in the hallway. "That's funny," she thought. "Where is everybody?" She unlocked the door to her room and opened it. She expected to see Kim, her roommate, but the room was dark. She reached to her right to turn on the lamp on her desk, but her hand only brushed the air. The lamp was gone. "That's strange," she thought. She turned to the left and dropped her books on the chair that was always by the door. This time, she heard her books fall to the floor. The chair wasn't there either. Now seriously worried, Laura reached for the light switch on the wall to her left. When the light came on, she gasped!

The Lizard

One afternoon when Mike was reading in his room, his mother suddenly screamed. Then she shouted, "Mike, come to the kitchen quickly! There's a lizard on the wall. You know I hate lizards in my kitchen. Kill it for me." Mike's mother ran out of the kitchen when Mike ran into it. On the wall was a small, light-brown lizard. He made a grab for it and caught it in his hand.

"Oh, Mike," said the lizard, "please don't kill me."

"Sorry," said Mike, "but my mother wants me to."

"I'm a magic lizard. I will give you three wishes if you don't kill me," said the little lizard.

"I don't believe you, but here is my first wish. I want a sports car in this kitchen right now." Mike looked at the lizard, who closed his eyes tightly.

Nothing happened.

Mike said, "I knew you weren't a magic lizard. Now I have to obey my mother's wish and kill you."

"Oh, please, no!" cried the lizard. "It's true that I am not magic, but if you save my life now, I will save yours some day."

Mike laughed, but he took the lizard outside and let him go. Mike didn't believe that the lizard could save his life, but one day, many years later, the lizard did. This is how it happened.

II PREPARING THE FIRST DRAFT

A Organize your ideas

Read over the list of ideas and words that you made when your group was talking. Brainstorm about how you want to end the story. If you are having trouble writing an ending, ask yourself the following questions.

1 What is the problem to be solved in this story?
2 What are some ways to solve that problem?
3 Do I want to write a scary story, a funny story, or an adventure story?
4 Do I need to add any new characters to the story? (Characters are people or animals in a story.) How will a new character change the story?

B Plan your writing

When you tell a story, you need to organize your ideas using time order. On your list, put a number *1* next to the first thing that happens in your story. Put a number *2* next to the second thing that happens, and so on.

C Write the first draft

Write your ending to the story that you chose. Have fun!

A Analyze a paragraph

Read the following ending that a student wrote to Story 3, "The Lizard." Answer the questions with your class.

1 What do you like about this story ending?

2 Are all of the sentences relevant to the story?

3 Are the sentences in a good order?

4 Did the writer use enough transitions?

5 Did the writer give enough details?

6 Does the paragraph have a good ending sentence?

> Mike was walking down the road. It had rained the night before, and the road was wet. He was going to meet a friend. While he was walking, he heard a small voice call him. He stopped and looked all around, but he couldn't find where the voice was coming from. He started to walk again. After a little while, he heard the same voice again. The voice came from near his feet. He saw a small hole. In the hole was the lizard. The lizard called to him. Mike bent down to hear the lizard's voice. When he bent down, a gunshot passed over his head. The lizard said to him, "I saved your life!" The lizard saved his life in the end.

B Revise your writing

To help each other revise your stories, you will read each other's paragraphs, and think about other details that you would like to know. Work in a small group, and follow these steps.

1 Collect all the papers from your group, and exchange them with another group.

2 Each person in your group will read all of the story endings. For each paper, do the following:

- Put a star next to one word, sentence, or detail that you like.
- If you do not understand a sentence, put a question mark (?) next to it.
- At the bottom of the paper, write one question about the story. Ask for more details about something in the paragraph, for example.

Your turn ⌁

When you get your paragraph back, reread it. Then answer these questions.

1 Are there any question marks on it? If there are, rewrite those sentences more clearly.
2 Answer the questions on the bottom of your paper. Can you add details to make your story better?
3 Ask yourself the questions in *Analyze a paragraph* on page 81. Do you need to make any changes?
4 Look at your *Progress Check* on page 76 of Chapter 5. Use it to help you revise your paragraph.

C Write the second draft

Rewrite your paragraph, and make any changes that you need. Write a title at the top of your paper.

IV | EDITING YOUR WRITING

A Focus on sentence grammar

Read these problem sentences taken from a student's ending for Story 1, "One Dark Night." Why are they a problem?

1 Because I was so happy to be out of the rain.
2 After I stood by the door for a few minutes.
3 Although I was terrified.
4 When I turned on my flashlight.
5 Before I could run.

> ### DEPENDENT CLAUSE FRAGMENTS
>
> The examples (1–5) above are a problem for the reader because they do not give enough information. They are incomplete and leave the reader with questions.
>
> 1 Because I was so happy to be out of the rain. (What happened?)
> 2 After I stood by the door for a few minutes. (What happened next?)
> 3 Although I was terrified. (What did the writer do?)
> 4 When I turned on my flashlight. (What did the writer see?)
> 5 Before I could run. (What happened before the writer could run?)
>
> Each of these examples is a dependent clause. We know that they are dependent clauses because each one begins with a subordinating conjunction. When a dependent clause stands by itself, it gives incomplete information. As we learned in previous chapters, an incomplete sentence is called a *fragment*. If you write a dependent clause as a separate sentence, it is a fragment, not a sentence.

Practice 1

Look at one student's ending to Story 2, "Mystery in the Dark." Write *F* above the fragments, and write a check (✓) above the good sentences. The first one is done for you.

> ✓
> ¹Laura gasped because her room was a mess! ²Then, she fainted. ³When she woke up. ⁴She started to put her things in their right places. ⁵After she finished cleaning up her room, she still couldn't find her desk anywhere. ⁶Just then, the girl in the next room came to Laura's room. ⁷She had lost her bed. ⁸While her roommate had lost a lamp. ⁹It was very strange because every person in the dorm had lost one thing. ¹⁰This dorm had one empty room. ¹¹Everybody went there because they wondered about what had happened in that room. ¹²They were surprised. ¹³When they opened the door. ¹⁴There were all the lost things! ¹⁵Since the students were very nervous. ¹⁶They grabbed their stuff and quickly left. ¹⁷After that, nothing like this ever happened in that dorm again. ¹⁸It is still a mystery.

CORRECTING A FRAGMENT

In a complex sentence, every dependent clause must be joined to an independent clause. A dependent clause standing by itself is a fragment. To correct a fragment, add an independent clause to the dependent clause, or join the dependent clause to an independent clause.

Fragment:	When his mother suddenly screamed.
Sentence:	Mike was reading in his room when his mother suddenly screamed.
Fragment:	As I walked. A strong wind blew buckets of rain.
Sentence:	As I walked, a strong wind blew buckets of rain.

Note that when the dependent clause comes first, it is followed by a comma. When it comes after the independent clause, do not use a comma.

Practice 2

Correct any fragments in the story in *Practice 1* by joining the fragments to sentences before or after them. Write the corrected sentences on a piece of paper. Remember to use the correct punctuation for complex sentences.

Practice 3

Add an independent clause to each of these dependent clauses to make a complex sentence. When you have finished, you will have an ending to the story "One Dark Night." (For the beginning of the story, see page 79.)

One Dark Night

1 Because I was so happy to be out of the rain, _____

_____

2 After I stood by the door for a few minutes, _____

_____

3 Although I was terrified, _____

_____

4 When I turned on my flashlight, _____

_____

5 Before I could run, _____

_____

6 When the door slammed shut, _____

_____

7 While I stood there without moving, _____

_____

8 After I stopped laughing, _____

_____

B Edit your writing

Use the *Editing Checklist* on the right to edit your paragraph. Follow these steps.

1 Underline all of the subjects in your sentences. Circle all of the verbs.
2 Using the checklist, look for only one kind of mistake at a time.
3 Use *Quick Check* on pages 123–140 to help you correct your mistakes.
4 Look at your *Progress Check* on page 76 of Chapter 5. Use it to help you edit your paragraph.

EDITING CHECKLIST ✔

Look at each sentence.

- ☐ **1** Does every sentence have a subject and a verb?
- ☐ **2** Are there any fragments?
- ☐ **3** Are there any run-on sentences?

Look at each verb.

- ☐ **4** Do all of the verbs agree with their subjects?
- ☐ **5** Are all of the verbs the correct tense and form?

Look at the punctuation and capitalization.

- ☐ **6** Does each sentence begin with a capital letter?
- ☐ **7** Does each sentence end with the correct punctuation?
- ☐ **8** Is there a comma after each transition?
- ☐ **9** Is there a comma in each compound sentence?
- ☐ **10** Are there commas where they are needed in complex sentences?

Look at the words.

- ☐ **11** Is each word spelled correctly?

C Write the final draft

Write your final draft, including your changes and corrections. Use correct format.

A Share your writing

Here is your chance to read the story endings written by some of your classmates.

1 Get in a group with classmates who wrote endings to the same story as you did. Collect all of the story endings in your group.

2 Exchange your group's story endings with another group.

3 Each person in your group will read all of the papers. Then, your group will decide which story ending is the most enjoyable to read.

4 Read to the class the ending chosen by your group. Then explain why you chose that story ending.

B Check your progress

After you get your paragraph back from your teacher, complete the *Progress Check* below.

PROGRESS CHECK

Date: _____

Paragraph title: _____

Things I did well in this paragraph:

_____

_____

_____

Things I need to work on in my next paragraph:

_____

_____

_____

Look at your *Progress Check* on page 76 of Chapter 5. How did you improve your writing in this paragraph?

_____

_____

_____

A Favorite Place

You probably have a favorite place, a place you love to be. Maybe you feel safe and peaceful in that place. Maybe it's an exciting place where you feel very much alive. Your favorite place may be a room, a park, a city street, a secret place in the woods, a beach, or a club. What is your favorite place?

In this chapter, you will write a paragraph describing your favorite place.

A Picture this

Answer the questions about each photograph with your class or in a small group.

1 Where is this place?
2 Do you like to be in this kind of place?
3 Do you have a favorite place like this?

B Get ideas

Follow the steps below to get ideas about your favorite place.

1 Draw a simple picture of your favorite place on a separate piece of paper. Try to put in as much detail as possible. If you do not want to draw a picture, you can make a word picture of the place. To make a word picture, write the names of objects on the paper in the same place that they would be if you were drawing a picture.

2 Brainstorm about the following questions. Write your ideas in words or phrases.
   - Why do you like this place?
   - What do you do there?
   - How you feel in this place?

II PREPARING THE FIRST DRAFT

A Organize your ideas

Read these two descriptions. Which one is easier to picture in your mind? Why? Discuss your answers with your class or in a small group.

Draft A

My favorite place is my bedroom because I can do anything I like there. My bed is under the window, so I can hear the birds in the morning. My desk is next to the door, but I rarely study there. Usually I sit on my bed to study. I have a beautiful, old chest of drawers with my jewelry box and bottles of perfume on it. Also, there is a fat, comfortable chair in my room. Sometimes I sit there to read, and sometimes I just throw my clothes on it. I love to listen to music in my room, too. I have a stereo. It is on a bookcase. Also, there is a mirror above the chest of drawers. Sometimes I stand in front of it and pretend that I am a singer in a rock band. Also, there is a basket for my cat to sleep in next to the bookcase. Finally, there is a nightstand next to my bed. It holds my clock radio, a few empty soda cans, and several empty plates with crumbs on them.

Draft B

My favorite place is my bedroom because I can do anything I like there. When you come into my room, my desk is on the right, next to the wall. It is completely covered with papers and books, so I rarely study there. In the corner is a fat, comfortable chair. Sometimes I sit there to read, and sometimes

continued

I just throw my clothes on it. In the middle of the next wall is a window, and my bed is under it. I love listening to the birds in the morning when I am still half asleep. Also, I usually study on my bed since my desk is such a mess. There is a nightstand to the right of the bed. It holds my clock radio, a few empty soda cans, and several empty plates with crumbs on them. In the middle of the next wall is a low bookcase with three shelves. My stereo is on the bookcase, and I love to listen to music when I am in my room. On the floor to the left of the bookcase is a basket for my cat to sleep in. Next to the basket is the door to my closet. In the middle of the wall across from my bed is a beautiful old chest of drawers with my jewelry box and bottles of perfume on it. There is a mirror above the chest. Sometimes I stand in front of it and pretend that I am a singer in a rock band. My room isn't very big, but I enjoy being in it very much.

DESCRIBING A PLACE

When you write a description about a place, you want your readers to be able to see the place in their minds as they read. To help the readers imagine your place, start with a beginning point.

<u>When you come into my room</u>, my desk is on the right, next to the wall.

Then use words to show the direction your description moves around the place.

There is a bookshelf <u>to the right of my desk</u>.

Your turn

On a separate piece of paper, draw a picture of the bedroom described in Draft B.

B Plan your writing

Look back at the picture you drew of your favorite place. Circle the spot in the picture where you will begin your description. Draw arrows to show the direction in which your description will move.

C Write the first draft

Write a paragraph about your favorite place. Use the picture or word picture that you drew in *Get ideas* on page 89. Remember to describe what you do and how you feel in this place, not just the things there. Also remember that readers should be able to see your place in their minds while they read your paragraph.

A Analyze a paragraph

Read the following paragraph. This student describes a very large place, so the description is a little different than for a small place. Answer the questions with your class.

1 What do you like about this paragraph?
2 Is the paragraph about one main idea?
3 Is there a good topic sentence?
4 Are all of the supporting sentences relevant to the main idea?
5 Is the place description organized clearly? Can you picture the place in your mind?
6 Did the writer give enough details?
7 Does the paragraph have a good conclusion?

The Desert

I love the desert because it makes me feel spiritual. I especially like the sunrise and sunset in the desert. In my country, Saudi Arabia, I go to the desert on the weekend to relax. I leave my city, Riyadh, and drive to the desert alone. Then, when I arrive at the desert in the evening, I walk. I listen to the birds in the bushes and small trees. I look at the tall sand dunes, and I look far away to the hills. In the desert, there is so much space. I can see for 40 kilometers. I look at everything around me, especially the orange and red sunset. When the night comes, I feel relaxed. Then, I look at the sky and the stars in the sky. I can't forget the beautiful sky. Finally, I feel happy, and I feel close to God in that beautiful picture. I lay my blankets on the sand, build a fire, and eat some dinner. I make Arabian coffee. Then, I go to bed because I am waiting for another beautiful picture in the morning. I mean the sunrise.

B Revise your writing

Exchange the first draft of your paragraph with a partner. Read your partner's paragraph, and then follow these steps.

1 Draw a picture of your partner's favorite place.
2 Put an *X* at the starting place of the description.
3 Draw arrows to show the direction in which the description goes.
4 Under the picture, write two words to describe how your partner feels in this place.

Your turn

Get your paragraph back from your partner. Reread your paragraph, and answer the questions.

1 Was your partner able to draw a clear picture from your paragraph?
2 Did your partner understand how you feel in this place? If not, talk to your partner, and find out what was not clear in your paragraph.
3 Ask yourself the questions in *Analyze a paragraph* on page 91. Do you need to make any changes?
4 Look at your *Progress Check* on page 86 of Chapter 6. Use it to help you revise your paragraph.

C Write the second draft

Rewrite your paragraph, and make any changes that you need. Write a title at the top of your paper.

IV EDITING YOUR WRITING

A Focus on sentence grammar

PREPOSITIONS OF PLACE

When you describe a place, you need to use *prepositions* to tell where things are. The sentences on the next page use prepositions of place to describe the town.

Between	A house stands <u>between</u> two trees.
In front of	<u>In front of</u> the house, there are two children and a dog.
On	The children and the dog are sitting <u>on</u> the grass.
Next to / beside	The boy is <u>next to</u> the girl, and the dog is <u>beside</u> the girl.
In	A car is <u>in</u> the driveway. A boat is <u>in</u> the river.
Over / above	A bridge crosses <u>over</u> the river, and birds are flying <u>above</u> the bridge.
Under / below	The person <u>under</u> the car is fixing it. The river is <u>below</u> the bridge.
In the middle of	A car is <u>in the middle of</u> the bridge.
Behind	A truck is <u>behind</u> the car.
Across from	There are some stores <u>across</u> the bridge <u>from</u> the house. There is a gas station <u>across from</u> the stores.
To the right of	A drug store is <u>to the right of</u> the grocery store.
To the left of	A furniture store stands <u>to the left of</u> the grocery store.

Practice 1

Look at the picture, and fill in the paragraph on page 94 with the correct prepositions.

The Kitchen

This is a picture of Kristen and Matt's kitchen. Kristen is sitting
_____ (1) a chair with her breakfast _____ (2) her. Her
napkin is _____ (3) the fork, and the plate is _____ (4)
the fork and the knife. A fruit bowl is _____ (5) the table. Matt is
making his breakfast at the stove, and the kitchen table is _____ (6)
him. The cat is sitting _____ (7) the floor near the stove. A plant is
hanging _____ (8) the sink. The dish drainer is _____ (9)
the sink, and a teapot is _____ (10) the sink. _____ (11)
the counter, there are some cabinets for the dishes. The toaster is
_____ (12) the refrigerator. The trash can is _____ (13) the
wall and _____ (14) the stove.

Practice 2

Write sentences about the kitchen using the words given.

1 the pot / the stove

The pot is on the stove.

2 a cabinet / the dish drainer

_____

3 some dishes / the dish drainer

_____

4 the paper towel roll / the counter

_____

5 Kristen / Matt

_____

6 the teapot / the toaster

_____

7 the toaster / the refrigerator / the teapot

_____

8 the coffee cups / the cabinet

_____

Your turn ↺

Exchange the second draft of your paragraph with a partner. Draw your partner's favorite place. Then return the paragraph and drawing. Look at your partner's drawing of your favorite place. Talk to your partner and find out what was not clear in your description. Make any changes that you need to so that the reader can picture your place clearly.

B Edit your writing

Use the *Editing Checklist* to edit your paragraph. Follow these steps.

1 Underline all of the subjects in your sentences. Circle all of the verbs.

2 Using the checklist, look for only one kind of mistake at a time.

3 Check your paragraph for prepositions. Have you used them correctly? Change or add where necessary.

4 Use *Quick Check* on pages 123–140 to help you fix your mistakes.

5 Look at your *Progress Check* on page 86 of Chapter 6. Use it to help you edit your paragraph.

EDITING CHECKLIST ☑

Look at each sentence.

☐ 1 Does every sentence have a subject and a verb?

☐ 2 Are there any fragments?

☐ 3 Are there any run-on sentences?

Look at each verb.

☐ 4 Do all of the verbs agree with their subjects?

☐ 5 Are all of the verbs the correct tense and form?

Look at the punctuation and capitalization.

☐ 6 Does each sentence begin with a capital letter?

☐ 7 Does each sentence end with the correct punctuation?

☐ 8 Is there a comma after each transition?

☐ 9 Is there a comma in each compound sentence?

☐ 10 Are there commas where they are needed in complex sentences?

Look at the words.

☐ 11 Are prepositions used correctly?

☐ 12 Is each word spelled correctly?

C Write the final draft

Write your final draft, including your changes and corrections. Use correct format.

A Share your writing

Your teacher will choose some papers to read aloud. Listen and try to picture the place in your mind. Ask the writer any questions you have about the place.

B Check your progress

After you get your paragraph back from your teacher, complete the *Progress Check* below.

PROGRESS CHECK

Date: _____

Paragraph title: _____

Things I did well in this paragraph:

_____

_____

_____

Things I need to work on in my next paragraph:

_____

_____

_____

Look at your *Progress Check* on page 86 of Chapter 6. How did you improve your writing in this paragraph?

_____

_____

_____

The Ideal Spouse

Are you married or single? If you are single, maybe you would like to marry soon. Or, maybe you think, "Married? Not for a long time!" If you are married, you probably have thoughts about marriage to share. What makes an ideal spouse? Most people agree that the inside of a person, his or her personality, is the most important thing for a happy marriage.

In this chapter, you will write about your ideal or real spouse.

A Picture this

Answer the questions about each photograph with your class or in a small group.

1 How would you describe each couple?
2 What do you think they are they feeling?
3 Does this couple remind you of a couple you know?

B Get ideas

Look at this list of adjectives. Each adjective below describes a quality. A person's personality is made up of many qualities. With your class, talk about what these words mean. Then, circle four adjectives to describe your ideal spouse or your real spouse.

cheerful	faithful	honest	self-confident	brave
funny	intelligent	warm	ambitious	thoughtful
gentle	kind	creative	responsible	curious

FREEWRITING

Freewriting is a good way to get ideas for your paragraph about your real or ideal spouse. *Freewriting* is like brainstorming because you try to write down as many ideas as possible. But in freewriting, you write in paragraph form, not in list form.

This is how freewriting works.

- Your teacher will give you about five or ten minutes. In that time, you write as much as you can about your topic without stopping.

- Write sentences, questions, words, or phrases. Do not worry about grammar or spelling. Also, you may write a word in your own native language if you do not know it in English, but try not to do this very often.

- Keep writing for the whole time that the teacher gives you. Do not stop writing, and do not erase. If you cannot think of anything to say, write the same word again and again, or write your topic. Soon, you will have a new idea.

- After you finish freewriting, read what you have written. Underline any ideas that you want to use in your paragraph. You can add any new ideas that you think of.

Here is an example of freewriting. It is written in paragraph form, but has many errors. This is not something to worry about when you are freewriting.

> My ideal spouse. I don't want to married now. Maybe some time. Beautiful! Beautiful! Funny, too. Why funny important for me? I like to laugh. I want to have much laughing in my house. Not crying. Girls cry too much. Not like guys. What other thing? wife wife wife Yes. I want responsible, not same as aunt. She spend uncle money, don't pay bills. Uncle not happy.

Your turn ↝

Freewrite about your ideal or real spouse. Write about the qualities you have chosen. Why do you think they are important in a husband or wife?

A Organize your ideas

Read your freewriting. Which qualities of a spouse did you write about? Which quality is most important to you?

ORGANIZING BY IMPORTANCE

Writing about ideas in order of importance is one way to organize ideas in a logical order. *Logical order* means explaining your reasons in a clear way so the reader can follow your thinking. If your ideas are all mixed up, the reader will not understand them.

When you write about the qualities of your real or ideal spouse, you can organize them from most important to least important or from least important to most important.

Read these two drafts, and follow the steps below each one.

Draft A

Choosing a Husband

I am only 20 years old now, and I am enjoying life as a student. I don't think about marriage very often. But I am sure that someday I will get married. I hope that my future husband will have certain qualities. First, the man that I want to marry will be intelligent. Intelligent men are more interesting to me than dull men. I don't want to be bored by my husband. Second, it is important for him to be a kind man. I want him to be kind and helpful both to me and to other people. A kind man will care about me and try to make my life better. Life is easier and more enjoyable when you have a kind spouse. Next, I want my husband to be honest. If he is honest, I can always believe him, and our communication will be better. If a man is dishonest or keeps secrets from me, I will always be unsure of his love and worried about our marriage. Most of all, I want a faithful husband. I need to trust that he will always stay true to me physically and in his heart. A good marriage needs complete trust, and for that, I need a faithful husband. If my real husband has all the qualities of my ideal husband, we will have a wonderful marriage.

---

1 Circle the transitions in Draft A that come before each quality.

2 Circle the letter of the sentence that describes Draft A.

   a This paragraph is organized from most important to least important.

   b This paragraph is organized from least important to most important.

Draft B

Choosing a Husband

I am only 20 years old now, and I am enjoying my life as a student. I don't think about marriage very often. But I am sure that someday I will get married. I hope that my future husband will have certain qualities. Most important, I want a faithful husband. I need to trust that he will always stay true to me physically and stay true in his heart. A good marriage needs complete trust, and for that, I need a faithful husband. Also, I want my husband to be honest. If he is honest, I can always believe him, and our communication will be better. If a man is dishonest or keeps secrets from me, I will always be unsure of his love and worried about our marriage. In addition, it is important for him to be a kind man. I want him to be kind and helpful both to me and to other people. A kind man will care about me and try to make my life better. Life is easier and more enjoyable when you have a kind spouse. Finally, the man that I want to marry will be intelligent because intelligent men are more interesting to me than dull men. I don't want to be bored by my husband. If my real husband has all the qualities of my ideal husband, we will have a wonderful marriage.

1 Circle the transitions in Draft B that come before each quality.

2 Circle the letter of the sentence that describes Draft B.

   a This paragraph is organized from most important to least important.

   b This paragraph is organized from least important to most important.

3 Which order do you prefer, the order used in Draft A or Draft B? Why?

B Plan your writing

Look at the four qualities you circled in *Get ideas* on page 99. On the lines below, write the four qualities that you have chosen to describe your ideal or real spouse. Put them in a logical order. Then, circle the phrase that describes the order you are using.

1 _____

2 _____

3 _____

4 _____

Most important to least important

Least important to most important

TRANSITIONS

In your paragraph, you will write about four qualities in order of importance. Of course, in a paragraph, you do not use numbers to list these four qualities. Instead, you use transition words and phrases. These transitions show when the writer is going to introduce a new quality. Read the transitions below. Notice that transitions are followed by a comma.

First,	Also,	Finally,
First of all,	In addition,	Most of all,
Second,	Moreover,	Most important,
Third,	Next,	

With your class, look at Drafts A and B again. Which transitions are used in Draft A? Which are used in Draft B? Which transitions introduce the quality of greatest importance?

Practice 1

Read the paragraph below. Underline each of the four qualities. Then add a transition to introduce each quality.

My Future Wife

¹When I close my eyes, I can see my future wife. ²She will look beautiful, of course! ³But she will also have many beautiful qualities on the inside. ⁴She will be a cheerful person. ⁵I am a pessimist, so I want a wife to smile at me and make me happy. ⁶I like to hear laughter in the house. ⁷I want a self-confident wife. ⁸If she has confidence in herself, she will not be afraid to try new things, and she will succeed. ⁹If she fails, she will not be afraid to try again. ¹⁰She will be gentle. ¹¹When I have a hard day at work, I want to come home to a gentle wife. ¹²Her soft way will make me feel better. ¹³I think children need a gentle mother. ¹⁴My wife will always be faithful to me. ¹⁵I want her to love only me and not look at any other man. ¹⁶Then, our hearts will be safe.

C Write the first draft

Write a paragraph describing the personality of your ideal spouse. Include the reasons you chose each quality. Introduce each quality with a transition.

III REVISING YOUR WRITING

A Analyze a paragraph

Read the following student paragraph. Answer the questions with your class.

1 What do you like about this paragraph?
2 Is the paragraph about one main idea?
3 Is there a good topic sentence?
4 Are all of the supporting sentences relevant to the main idea?
5 Are the supporting sentences in a good order?
6 Did the writer use enough transitions?
7 Did the writer explain why each quality is important?
8 Does the paragraph have a good conclusion?

A Good Life Partner

My husband is a very good man. First of all, he is loving. He loves animals, flowers, and people. He has a lot of flowers and pictures of animals at our home. He especially loves wolves and whales. Also, he is very energetic, so he loves to play tennis and to scuba dive. He likes to swim in the ocean, too, but he can't because we live far away from the beach. He is very careful while driving. He likes to shop, so we often go to the mall. He is very happy when he buys new things. Finally, he is very helpful. He usually helps me with the housework. Sometimes he cooks, and sometimes he washes our clothes. He is a very good life partner, so I love him very much.

B Revise your writing

Exchange first drafts with a partner. Read your partner's paragraph, and answer these questions about it.

1 What do you like about your partner's paper? Put a star next to any ideas or sentences that you like.

2 List the qualities your partner wants in a spouse.

a _____

b _____

c _____

d _____

3 Circle the phrase that describes how your partner organized the qualities.

Most important to least important

Least important to most important

4 Does a transition introduce each quality?

5 How did you know which was the most important quality?

Your turn

Get your draft back from your partner. Reread your paragraph, and answer these questions.

1 Was your organization clear so that your partner could understand it?

2 Ask yourself the questions in *Analyze a paragraph* on page 103 about your own paragraph. Do you need to make any more changes?

3 Look at your *Progress Check* on page 96 of Chapter 7. Use it to help you revise your paragraph.

C Write the second draft

Rewrite your paragraph, and make any changes that you need. Write a title at the top of your paper.

IV EDITING YOUR WRITING

A Focus on sentence grammar

You have learned about three kinds of sentences: simple, compound, and complex. Which is the best kind of sentence to use in your writing? Read the three drafts of a paragraph below, and answer the question or questions after each one.

Draft A

> Ernest is my wonderful husband. He always talks with a smile. His smile makes me laugh all the time. He is a very funny and carefree person. We have free time sometimes. Then, we play together like children. He is also a responsible person. He is a good man. He cares for me and our house. He always pays the bills.

1 What kind of sentences are used in Draft A: simple, compound, or complex?

Draft B

> I love Ernest very much because he is a wonderful husband. Since he is a happy person, he always talks with a smile. When he smiles, I laugh. We play together like children when we have free time because he is a funny and carefree person. Because he is a responsible person, I think that he is a good man. Because he cares for me and our house, he always pays the bills.

2 What kind of sentences are used in Draft B: simple, compound, or complex?

Draft C

> Ernest is a wonderful husband, so I love him very much. He always talks with a smile, and his smile makes me laugh all the time. He is very funny, and he is a carefree person. We have free time sometimes, and then we play like children. He is also a responsible person, and he is a good man. He cares for me and our house, so he always pays the bills.

3 What kind of sentences are used in Draft C: simple, compound, or complex?

4 Is it best to use one kind of sentence in a paragraph?

SENTENCE VARIETY

An English proverb says, "Variety is the spice of life." What do you think this proverb means? *Variety* means a mix of different things. Spices are items such as salt and pepper, which we add to food to make it taste better. Using different spices in food makes eating more interesting. Good writing is the same. A paragraph is more interesting to read when a variety of sentences is used.

There are several ways to add variety to your paragraph.

- Join two sentences to make a different kind of sentence.

    We have free time sometimes. Then, we play like children.

    When we have free time, we play like children.

- Start a sentence with a transition (*then, second, after that,* and so on).

    Also, Ernest is a responsible person and a good man.

- Start a sentence with a phrase (*at night, in school, every day,* and so on).

    In fact, he is a very funny and carefree person.

Read Draft D of the paragraph about Ernest. Now there is a variety of sentences and transitions. Do you agree that this draft is more enjoyable to read?

Draft D

> Ernest is my wonderful husband. He always talks with a smile, and his smile makes me laugh all the time. In fact, he is a very funny and carefree person. When we have free time, we play together like children. Also, Ernest is a responsible person and a good man. Because he cares for me and our house, he always pays the bills.

Practice 2

Rewrite each group of sentences. Join them or separate them to make different kinds of sentences. Add transitions and move prepositional phrases to vary the sentences. The first one has been done for you.

1 I am a night person. I want to marry another night person. I hate cheerfulness in the morning!

I am a night person, so I want to marry another night person. I hate

cheerfulness in the morning!

2 I don't like to talk in the morning. I don't have enough energy to be pleasant. I want to be grumpy and silent.

_____

_____

_____

3 I shouldn't marry a morning person. If my wife chatters in the morning, I will go crazy.

_____

_____

_____

4 I need to marry a night person. Another night person will frown at me in the morning. She'll leave me alone. She will understand me.

_____

_____

_____

5 In my opinion, night people should marry night people. Morning people should marry morning people. They will be happier that way.

_____

_____

_____

Your turn

Look at your second draft. Choose one of the qualities of your ideal spouse. Find the sentences that you wrote for that quality. On the lines below, rewrite these sentences in different ways. You can combine some of the sentences or make longer sentences into shorter ones. You can also add transitions or prepositional phrases at the beginning of some of the sentences. Then choose the sentences you want to use in your final draft.

_____

_____

_____

_____

_____

_____

B Edit your writing

Use the *Editing Checklist* to edit your paragraph. Follow these steps.

1 Rewrite sentences in your paragraph to make them more interesting. Check that you have a variety of sentences.

2 Use the *Editing Checklist* below to continue editing your paragraph. Use *Quick Check* on pages 123–140 to help you fix your mistakes.

3 Look at your *Progress Check* on page 96 of Chapter 7. Use it to help you edit your paragraph.

EDITING CHECKLIST ☑

Look at each sentence.

☐ 1 Does every sentence have a subject and a verb?

☐ 2 Are there any fragments?

☐ 3 Are there any run-on sentences?

☐ 4 Is there a variety of sentences?

Look at each verb.

☐ 5 Do all of the verbs agree with their subjects?

☐ 6 Are all of the verbs in the correct tense and form?

Look at the punctuation and capitalization.

☐ 7 Does each sentence begin with a capital letter?

☐ 8 Does each sentence end with the correct punctuation?

☐ 9 Is there a comma after each transition?

☐ 10 Is there a comma in each compound sentence?

☐ 11 Are there commas where they are needed in complex sentences?

Look at the words.

☐ 12 Are prepositions used correctly?

☐ 13 Is each word spelled correctly?

C Write the final draft

Write your final draft, including your changes and corrections. Use correct format.

V FOLLOWING UP

A Share your writing

Exchange papers with a partner, and read each other's paragraphs. Talk about your papers. Compare your ideal or real spouses. How are they the same or different? Ask each other any questions you have about the papers.

B Check your progress

After you get your paragraph back from your teacher, complete the *Progress Check* below.

PROGRESS CHECK

Date: _____

Paragraph title: _____

Things I did well in this paragraph:

_____

_____

_____

Things I need to work on in my next paragraph:

_____

_____

_____

Look at your *Progress Check* on page 96 of Chapter 7. How did you improve your writing in this paragraph?

_____

_____

_____

What's Your Opinion?

Y ou are sitting around with your friends after class, having a soda and eating a snack. Someone brings up a controversial subject, and soon everyone is part of a heated discussion. Some people raise their voices, and some even get angry. Everyone wants to express an opinion. Has this ever happened to you? Most people enjoy discussing their opinions.

In this chapter, you will write a paragraph that expresses one of your opinions.

A Picture this

Answer the questions about each photograph with your class or in a small group.

1 What is happening in the photograph?
2 What controversy does the photograph show?
3 Do you have a strong opinion about the activity in the photograph?

B Get ideas

Here are some opinions for you to think about and discuss with your classmates. First, read each opinion, and check (✓) whether you agree or disagree. Then, discuss your opinions with the class.

Agree	Disagree	Opinions
		1 I believe ghosts exist.
		2 Women should serve in the military.
		3 Couples should not live together before they get married.
		4 Baseball is more interesting than soccer.
		5 Computers have made our lives worse.
		6 Men should take three months off from work when their children are born.
		7 UFOs have visited our planet.
		8 Life in our world today is better than it was 50 years ago.

Follow these steps to get ideas for your paragraph.

1 Choose one opinion to write about, either from the ones above or another opinion that you feel strongly about.
2 Freewrite for five or ten minutes, as you did in Chapter 8 on page 99. While you write, think about all of your reasons for holding your opinion. What information do you have to support your reasons? Write as much as you can without stopping.
3 Read what you have written. If you think of any new ideas, add them to your freewriting.

▌II PREPARING THE FIRST DRAFT

A Organize your ideas

Practice ▮1▮

When you write your opinion, you want your reader to understand why you hold that opinion. You have to organize your ideas in a paragraph to help a reader understand your thinking. Read the following opinion paragraph, and look at the way the ideas are organized. Then, answer the questions that follow with your class.

Television: Not a Bad Idea

Although some parents don't allow their children to watch television, I believe that television can be good for families. First of all, television is inexpensive entertainment for families with young children. On a rainy afternoon, if it is too expensive to take the whole family to the movie theater, the family can sit in their living room with bowls of homemade popcorn and watch a movie on television. Second, television can be a good teacher. For example, small children can learn many things, such as the alphabet and numbers, on children's programs. In addition, nature programs teach them about our earth and how to care for it. Parents can also use television dramas as a way to start conversations with their children about important ideas. Most important, television lets children see a bigger picture of the world than their own small neighborhood. Our family cannot travel all over the globe, so the news shows them views of other people and places. The television also brings other cultures into our home through special children's programs. In conclusion, although some parents are throwing out their televisions, our family is keeping ours.

---

1 What is the writer's opinion? How do you know it is an opinion?

_____

_____

2 In which sentence do you find the opinion?

_____

_____

3 How many reasons does the writer give for the opinion? What are they?

_____

_____

_____

4 Where do you find the most important reason?

_____

_____

5 Why is it necessary to support an opinion with reasons?

_____

_____

6 What facts or examples does the writer use to support each reason?

_____

_____

7 Why is it necessary to support reasons with facts or examples?

_____

_____

8 What kind of sentence comes at the end of the composition? What does it do?

_____

_____

OUTLINES

When you write an opinion, you need to support it with several reasons. Each reason needs to be supported by facts or examples. After you decide on your reasons, facts, and examples, you need to arrange them in a clear order.

One way to organize your ideas is by using an outline. An *outline* is like the skeleton of a paragraph's ideas. You do not need to write the ideas in sentences. Use only words or phrases to remind yourself of your ideas.

Here is the beginning of an outline.

Outline for "Television: Not a Bad Idea"

Opinion: *television can be good for families*

Reason 1
– *inexpensive entertainment for families with young children*

    Support
    – *too expensive to take the whole family to a movie theater*

Practice 2

With a partner, read the following paragraph. Then, circle the opinion and underline the three reasons. Talk about the support for each reason.

Studying a Foreign Language

I believe that all students in all countries should study a foreign language. First, knowing another language can help you in your life. If you speak more than one language, you have a better chance for a good job. Many businesses today deal with companies in other countries, and they need workers who can speak another language. Also, your life can be more interesting and exciting when you can talk to people from other countries, read their books, watch their movies, and sing their songs. Second, when you study another language, you learn about the world and its cultures. A language is not separate from the people who speak it. When you learn a language, you learn more than words. You also learn how other people think and live. In our small world today, it is very important for world peace that we understand each other. Finally, when you study a different language, you learn about yourself. Learning another language gives you the chance to look at your own language and culture through someone else's eyes. For example, English uses only one word for *you*. When an American studies Spanish and learns that Spanish has two words for *you*, the American may ask, "Why does English have only one word for *you*?" The American is learning about his or her own culture. For all these reasons, I think that the world would be a better place if all students everywhere studied a foreign language.

Practice 3

Complete the outline for the paragraph on the opposite page.

Outline for "Studying a Foreign Language"

Opinion

Reason 1
– can help you in your life

    Support
    – you have a better chance for a good job
    – your life can be more interesting and exciting

Reason 2

    Support

Reason 3

    Support

Conclusion

B Plan your writing

Think about the opinion you chose to write about on page 113. Reread your freewriting, and underline all of the reasons for your opinion. Look for any facts or examples that support your reasons in your freewriting. Then, make an outline for your paragraph. Add more reasons if you need to.

<table>
<tr><td colspan="2" align="center">Paragraph Outline</td></tr>
<tr><td colspan="2">Opinion

</td></tr>
<tr><td colspan="2">Reason 1

    Support

</td></tr>
<tr><td colspan="2">Reason 2

    Support

</td></tr>
<tr><td colspan="2">Reason 3

    Support

</td></tr>
<tr><td colspan="2">Conclusion

</td></tr>
</table>

C Write the first draft

Write your paragraph, following your outline. Explain your thinking clearly so that the reader can understand why you hold your opinion.

III REVISING YOUR WRITING

A Analyze a paragraph

Exchange drafts with a partner. Outline your partner's paragraph on a separate piece of paper. Then, answer the questions.

1 What is your partner's opinion?
2 Did the writer give enough reasons for you?
3 Do all of the reasons support the opinion?
4 Is each reason supported by facts or examples?
5 Does the paragraph need any more transitions?
6 Is there anything you do not understand?
7 Did the writer give a strong explanation for his or her opinion?

B Revise your writing

Follow these steps to revise your writing.

1 Get together with your partner. Talk about the outlines you both made and your answers to the questions. Do you need to add or change anything to make your explanation of your opinion stronger?
2 Look at your *Progress Check* on page 109 of Chapter 8. Use it to help you revise your paragraph.

C Write the second draft

Rewrite your paragraph and make any changes that you need. Write a title at the top of your paper.

IV EDITING YOUR WRITING

A Focus on sentence grammar

To be a good writer, you need to be able to edit your own work. You have learned about many different things to check for when you edit your writing. When you are writing on your own, you need to remember those things and edit for them.

Your turn ↩

Make your own editing checklist. Try to remember everything that you checked for in Chapters 1–8. Do not look back at previous chapters!

PERSONAL EDITING CHECKLIST ✓

Look at each sentence.

Look at each verb.

Look at the punctuation and capitalization.

Look at the words.

B Edit your writing

1 As a class, compare your editing checklists. Then, with your class, fill in the *Class Editing Checklist* below. Use it to check your own paper.

2 Look at your *Progress Check* on page 109 of Chapter 8. Use it to help you edit your paragraph.

CLASS EDITING CHECKLIST ✔

Look at each sentence.

Look at each verb.

Look at the punctuation and capitalization.

Look at the words.

C Write the final draft

Write your final draft, including your changes and corrections. Use correct format.

A Share your writing

Follow these steps to share your writing.

1 Get in a small group. If possible, work with others who wrote about the same opinion that you did.
2 Exchange papers with another group.
3 Each person in the group will read all of the papers. Then, the group will decide which paragraph made the strongest explanation of the opinion.
4 The teacher will read each group's chosen paragraph. The group will explain why they chose that paragraph.

B Check your progress

After you get your paragraph back from your teacher, complete the *Progress Check* below.

PROGRESS CHECK

Date: _____

Paragraph title: _____

Things I did well in this paragraph:

_____

_____

_____

Things I need to work on in my next paragraph:

_____

_____

_____

Look at your *Progress Checks* from previous chapters. How did you improve your writing in this paragraph?

_____

_____

_____

Quick Check

This guide will help you check and edit your writing. It explains common editing marks and shows you how to correct errors. You can use it to edit your work after you write or to help you fix your mistakes after your teacher returns your paragraph to you.

I EDITING SYMBOLS

When your teacher returns your paragraph to you, your errors may be marked with the editing symbols shown here.

V = verb problem

S-V = subject-verb agreement

Frag = sentence fragment

RO = run-on sentence

WF = word form

WW = wrong word

SP = spelling

P = punctuation

C = capitalization

Quick Check has a section for each of the editing symbols. You can refer to those sections to learn more about how to correct common errors.

Section in Quick Check	Symbol	Wrong	Correct
A	V	V Yesterday, I eat breakfast early.	Yesterday, I ate breakfast early.
B	S-V	S-V She get up late every day.	She gets up late every day.
C	Frag	Frag We hungry in the morning.	We are hungry in the morning.
D	RO	RO I love Sunday mornings, I can sleep late.	I love Sunday mornings because I can sleep late.
E	WF	WF He is a happily man.	He is a happy man.
F	WW	WW She went at the morning.	She went in the morning.
G	SP	SP He drinks coffe for breakfast.	He drinks coffee for breakfast.
H	P	P Can you see the stars.	Can you see the stars?
I	C	C He gets up late on sundays.	He gets up late on Sundays.

A Verb problem (V)

1 Do I need to use the *simple present*?

Meaning	Verb form	Negative
a Use simple present for habitual actions. I sleep late every Saturday morning. **b** Use simple present for facts. They are brothers. I live in Toronto.	I, you, we, they *talk* He, she, it *talks*	*to do* + *not* + verb I, you, we, they *do not talk* He, she, it *does not talk*
	The verb *to be*	
	I *am* You, we, they *are* He, she, it *is*	I *am not* You, we, they *are not* He, she, it *is not*

2 Do I need to use the *present progressive*?

Meaning	Verb form	Negative
An event is happening at the time of speaking. Look! It is snowing.	*to be* + verb + *-ing* I *am talking* You, we, they *are talking* He, she, it *is talking*	*to be* + *not* + verb + *-ing* I *am not talking* You, we, they *are not talking* He, she, it *is not talking*

3 Do I need to use the *simple past*?

Meaning	Verb form	Negative
An event happened and finished in the past. I called her last night.	verb + *-ed* I, you, he, she, it, we, they *talked* (For irregular verbs, see the chart on the next page.)	*did* + *not* + verb I, you, he, she, it, we, they *did not talk*
	The verb *to be*	
	I, he, she, it *was* You, we, they *were*	I, he, she, it *was not* You, we, they *were not*

Common Irregular Verbs

Base form	Past	Past participle	Base form	Past	Past participle
be	was, were	been	hold	held	held
beat	beat	beaten	hurt	hurt	hurt
become	became	become	keep	kept	kept
begin	began	begun	know	knew	known
bend	bent	bent	leave	left	left
bet	bet	bet	let	let	let
bite	bit	bitten	lose	lost	lost
bleed	bled	bled	make	made	made
blow	blew	blown	meet	met	met
break	broke	broken	pay	paid	paid
bring	brought	brought	read	read	read
build	built	built	ride	rode	ridden
buy	bought	bought	ring	rang	rung
catch	caught	caught	run	ran	run
choose	chose	chosen	say	said	said
come	came	come	see	saw	seen
cost	cost	cost	sell	sold	sold
cut	cut	cut	send	sent	sent
dig	dug	dug	shake	shook	shaken
do	did	done	show	showed	shown
draw	drew	drawn	shut	shut	shut
drink	drank	drunk	sing	sang	sung
drive	drove	driven	sit	sat	sat
eat	ate	eaten	spend	spent	spent
fight	fought	fought	stand	stood	stood
find	found	found	steal	stole	stolen
fly	flew	flown	swim	swam	swum
forget	forgot	forgotten	take	took	taken
forgive	forgave	forgiven	teach	taught	taught
freeze	froze	frozen	tell	told	told
get	got	gotten	think	thought	thought
give	gave	given	throw	threw	thrown
go	went	gone	understand	understood	understood
have, has	had	had	wake	woke	woken
hear	heard	heard	wear	wore	worn
hide	hid	hidden	win	won	won
hit	hit	hit	write	wrote	written

4 Do I need to use the *present perfect*?

Meaning	Verb form	Negative
a An event happened in the past, but the time is not given. We have seen that movie. **b** An event began in the past and continues in the present. Ana has been here for six months.	*to have* + past participle I, you, we, they *have talked* He, she, it *has talked* (For irregular past participles, see the chart on the opposite page.)	*to have* + *not* + past participle I, you, we, they *have not talked* He, she, it *has not talked*

5 Do I need to use the *past progressive*?

Meaning	Verb form	Negative
An event was in progress at a specific time in the past. I was studying at 10 P.M. last night.	*was/were* + verb + *-ing* I, he, she, it *was talking* You, we, they *were talking*	*was/were* + *not* + verb + *-ing* I, he, she, it *was not talking* You, we, they *were not talking*

6 Do I need to use the *past perfect*?

Meaning	Verb form	Negative
An event happened in the past before another action or time in the past. They had left before I arrived. Nobody was there.	*had* + past participle I, you, he, she, it, we, they *had talked*	*had* + *not* + past participle I, you, he, she, it, we, they *had not talked*

7 Do I need to use the *simple future*?

Meaning	Verb form	Negative
An event is expected or planned to happen in the future. She will visit her friend tomorrow. She is going to visit her friend tomorrow.	**a** *will* + verb I, you, he, she, it, we, they *will talk* **b** *to be* + *going to* + verb I *am going to talk* You, we, they *are going to talk* He, she, it *is going to talk*	**a** *will* + *not* + verb I, you, he, she, it, we, they *will not talk* **b** *to be* + *not* + *going to* + verb I *am not going to talk* You, we, they *are not going to talk* He, she, it *is not going to talk*

B Subject-verb agreement (S-V)

Subject-verb agreement means that the verb is the correct form for the subject. When the verb is the correct form for the subject, we say the subject and the verb "agree." When the verb is not the correct form for the subject, we say they do not agree.

WRONG: I <u>is</u> here.
       (The subject and the verb do not agree.)

CORRECT: I <u>am</u> here.
       (The subject and verb agree.)

1 Do I need to add *-s* to the verb?

> In the simple present tense, *he, she,* and *it* need an *-s* at the end of the verb.
> WRONG: She <u>run</u> to the bus.
> CORRECT: She <u>runs</u> to the bus.

2 Is the subject a noncount noun?

> Noncount nouns are singular.
> WRONG: <u>Homeworks are</u> part of every student's life.
> CORRECT: <u>Homework is</u> part of every student's life.

3 Do all of the verbs agree with the subject?

When one subject has several verbs, all the verbs must agree with the subject.

WRONG: She goes outside and look at the stars.
CORRECT: She goes outside and looks at the stars.

4 Do I need *there is* or *there are*?

Use *there is* when the word after it is singular. Use *there are* when the word after it is plural.

There is a smile on her face.
There are smiles on their faces.

5 Is the subject a *singular* or *plural* word?

Certain words are singular, such as *each, every, everyone, everybody*.

Each child is special.
Every student hates homework.
Everyone wants to be happy.
Everybody needs food to live.

6 Does the verb agree with the *right word*?

The verb must agree with the subject, not the words after it.

WRONG: The students on the bus is going on the trip.
CORRECT: The students on the bus are going on the trip.
        (*The students* is the subject, not *the bus.*)

WRONG: One of the apples are bad.
CORRECT: One of the apples is bad.
        (*One* is the subject, not *the apples.*)

C Sentence fragment (Frag)

If a sentence does not have both a subject and a verb, it is called a fragment. A fragment is only part of a sentence, not a complete sentence.

1 How can I fix a *simple sentence fragment*?

> **a** Add a subject or a verb.
>
> FRAGMENT: Then, went to the store together.
> SENTENCE: Then, <u>they</u> went to the store together.
>
> FRAGMENT: Lucy and her cousin.
> SENTENCE: Lucy and her cousin <u>slept late</u>.
>
> **b** Add a subject and a verb.
>
> FRAGMENT: Difficult to spell English words.
> SENTENCE: <u>It is</u> difficult to spell English words.
>
> **c** Add the fragment to another sentence.
>
> FRAGMENT: And ate popcorn.
> SENTENCE: <u>We watched a movie</u> and ate popcorn.

2 How can I fix a *dependent clause fragment*?

> A dependent clause begins with a subordinating conjunction (*although, because, since, when, before, after, while*, etc.). A dependent clause cannot be a sentence by itself because it gives incomplete information. It must be joined to an independent clause to make a complex sentence.
>
> FRAGMENT: When the rain began.
> SENTENCE: <u>When the rain began</u>, <u>the children went inside</u>.
>   dependent clause   independent clause

D Run-on sentence (RO)

A run-on sentence happens when two simple sentences are run together without correct punctuation to separate them.

1 How can I fix a *run-on sentence*?

a If two independent clauses are run together and are not separated, you can make two simple sentences.

RUN-ON: John and Paul love soccer they often play after school.
CORRECT: John and Paul love soccer. They often play after school.

b If two independent clauses are only separated by a comma, you can make two simple sentences.

RUN-ON: John and Paul love soccer, they often play after school.
CORRECT: John and Paul love soccer. They often play after school.

c You can add a coordinating conjunction to make a compound sentence.

RUN-ON: John and Paul love soccer they often play after school.
CORRECT: John and Paul love soccer, <u>so</u> they often play after school.

d You can add a subordinating conjunction to make a complex sentence.

RUN-ON: John and Paul love soccer, they often play after school.
CORRECT: <u>Because</u> John and Paul love soccer, they often play after school.

2 How can I fix a *run-on compound sentence*?

A compound sentence does not usually have more than two independent clauses. If it has more than two independent clauses, it is probably a run-on sentence. To fix a run-on compound sentence, keep only two independent clauses in one sentence. Make a new sentence with any other independent clauses.

RUN-ON: <u>Laura wanted a job</u>, so <u>she applied at a fast food place</u>, and <u>now she works on weekends</u>.
              independent clause   independent clause   independent clause

CORRECT: Laura wanted a job, so she applied at a fast food place. Now she works on weekends.

E Word form (WF)

For many words in English, there are different forms of the word depending how the word is used. For example, a word can have different forms as a noun, a verb, an adjective, or an adverb. There is also a different form for plural nouns, past tense verbs, comparative adjectives, and so on.

1 Do I need the *noun* form?

a Use a noun for the subject or object of a verb.

WRONG: <u>Happy</u> is important to everyone.
CORRECT: <u>Happiness</u> is important to everyone.

b Use the noun form of a word when it is the object of a preposition.

WRONG: I was happy about my friend's <u>succeed</u>.
CORRECT: I was happy about my friend's <u>success</u>.

2 Do I need a *singular* or *plural* noun?

a Use a plural noun with plural words, such as *many* and *a few*.

WRONG: She always carries <u>many book</u>.
CORRECT: She always carries <u>many books</u>.

b Use a singular noun with singular words, such as *every* and *each*, and with noncount words (for example, *time, money, homework*).

WRONG: The teacher gave a paper to <u>every students</u>.
CORRECT: The teacher gave a paper to <u>every student</u>.
(*Every* is a singular word.)

WRONG: I hate <u>homeworks</u>!
CORRECT: I hate <u>homework</u>!
(*Homework* is a noncount noun. Noncount nouns are singular.)

3 Should I use an *adjective*?

a Use an adjective before a noun.

WRONG: He is a <u>health</u> baby.
CORRECT: He is a <u>healthy</u> baby.

b Use an adjective after the verb *to be* and linking verbs (for example, *to become, to seem, to look, to feel, to smell, to sound, to taste*).

WRONG: You look <u>terribly</u> today!
CORRECT: You look <u>terrible</u> today!

4 Should I use an *adverb*?

a Use an adverb to describe a verb.

WRONG: The rabbit jumped <u>quick</u> into its hole.

CORRECT: The rabbit jumped <u>quickly</u> into its hole.

b Use an adverb to describe an adjective.

WRONG: She is <u>terrible</u> sick.

CORRECT: She is <u>terribly</u> sick.

5 Which form of the adjective should I use when I compare things?

	Adjective	Comparative	Superlative
a adjectives with 1 syllable	old big	older than bigger than	the oldest the biggest
b adjectives with 2 syllables, ending in *-y*	heavy noisy	heavier than noisier than	the heaviest the noisiest
c adjectives with 2 or more syllables	beautiful expensive	more beautiful than more expensive than	the most beautiful the most expensive
d irregular adjectives	good bad	better than worse than	the best the worst

F Wrong word (WW)

1 Did I use the correct *preposition of time*?

Prepositions of time		
in	I sleep late <u>in</u> the morning.	*in + the morning*
	She goes to class <u>in</u> the afternoon	*in + the afternoon*
	We eat dinner <u>in</u> the evening.	*in + the evening*
	School begins <u>in</u> September.	*in + month*
	The days are shorter <u>in</u> winter.	*in + season*
	My son was born <u>in</u> 1992.	*in + year*
at	Everyone sleeps <u>at</u> night.	*at + night*
	They play soccer <u>at</u> 4:00.	*at + clock time*
	I eat lunch <u>at</u> noon.	*at + noon*
	He goes to bed <u>at</u> midnight.	*at + midnight*
on	I work <u>on</u> Saturday.	*on + day*
	We were married <u>on</u> August 11, 2004.	*on + date*
	He calls her <u>on</u> Sunday night.	*on + day + morning* *afternoon* *evening* *night*
from from/to	I will graduate four years <u>from</u> now. We study <u>from</u> 8:30 <u>to</u> 10:30 P.M.	*from + a beginning time* *from + a beginning time* *to + an ending time*
by	<u>By</u> noon, all of the players will be ready. (When *by* is used with a time word, it means before or no later than the time word.)	*by + a future time/day/date*

2 Did I use the correct *pronoun* or *possessive adjective*?

a Use a subject pronoun for the subject of the sentence.

<u>He</u> went to France.

b Use an object pronoun if it is the object of a verb or of a preposition.

Jason took <u>her</u> to the dance.
Jason took Janet to <u>it</u>.

c Use a possessive adjective before a noun to show possession.

I washed <u>my</u> car.

d Use a possessive pronoun to show possession.

I washed <u>mine</u>.

Subject pronoun	Object pronoun	Possessive adjective	Possessive pronoun
<u>I</u> know Jim.	Jim knows <u>me</u>.	That is <u>my</u> house.	That is <u>mine</u>.
<u>You</u> know Jim.	Jim knows <u>you</u>.	That is <u>your</u> house.	That is <u>yours</u>.
<u>He</u> knows Jim.	Jim knows <u>him</u>.	That is <u>his</u> house.	That is <u>his</u>.
<u>She</u> knows Jim.	Jim knows <u>her</u>.	That is <u>her</u> house.	That is <u>hers</u>.
<u>It</u> knows Jim.	Jim knows <u>it</u>.	That is <u>its</u> house.	That is <u>its</u>.
<u>We</u> know Jim.	Jim knows <u>us</u>.	That is <u>our</u> house.	That is <u>ours</u>.
<u>They</u> know Jim.	Jim knows <u>them</u>.	That is <u>their</u> house.	That is <u>theirs</u>.

3 Should I use *to be* or *to have*?

a Use *to be* with:

- adjectives

  Her sisters <u>are</u> <u>intelligent</u>.
  My father <u>is</u> <u>short</u>.

- nouns that describe the subject

  They <u>are</u> <u>doctors</u>.
  I <u>am</u> a <u>student</u>.

- numbers for age and height

  She <u>is</u> <u>24 years old</u>.
  He <u>is</u> over <u>six feet tall</u>.

b Use *to have* with:

- belongings

  I <u>have</u> a new <u>car</u>.
  She <u>has</u> three <u>brothers</u>.

- body parts

  He <u>has</u> brown <u>eyes</u>.
  They <u>have</u> big <u>feet</u>.

- health

  I <u>have</u> a <u>cold</u>.
  My mother <u>has</u> a <u>weak heart</u>.

G Spelling (SP)

1 Should I add -s or -es to verbs and nouns?

a For most words, add only -s. This is also the rule for words ending in -e.
   run – run**s**
   dance – dance**s**
   school – school**s**

b If the word ends in -s, -ss, -sh, -ch or -x, add -es.
   bus – bus**es**
   kiss – kiss**es**
   brush – brush**es**
   watch – watch**es**
   box – box**es**

c If the word ends with a vowel (a, e, i, o, u) + -y, add only -s.
   toy – toy**s**
   buy – buy**s**
   day – day**s**

d If the word ends with a consonant (all other letters) + -y, change the -y to -i and add -es.
   study – stud**ies**
   fly – fl**ies**

2 How do I add -ed and -ing to verbs?

a Verbs ending in -e

   • When adding the -ed ending, add only -d.
   smile – smile**d**
   hope – hope**d**

   • When adding the -ing ending, drop the -e and add -ing.
   smile – smil**ing**
   hope – hop**ing**

b Verbs ending in -y

   • When adding the -ed ending

   If there is a vowel (a, e, i, o, u) before the -y, keep the -y.
   stay – stay**ed**
   enjoy – enjoy**ed**

   If there is a consonant (all other letters) before the -y, change the -y to -i.
   cry – cr**ied**
   hurry – hurr**ied**

   • When adding the -ing ending, just add -ing to the end of the verb
   stay – stay**ing**
   cry – cry**ing**

3 When do I double the consonant when adding *-ed* or *-ing* to verbs?

a One-syllable verbs ending in a consonant

- If the verb ends in two consonants, add *-ed* or *-ing*.
  tal**k** – tal**ked** – tal**king**
     cc
  hel**p** – hel**ped** – hel**ping**
     cc

- If the verb ends in two vowels and a consonant, add *-ed* or *-ing*.
  w**ait** – wait**ed** – wait**ing**
     vvc
  p**our** – pour**ed** – pour**ing**
     vvc

- If the verb ends in a consonant, a vowel, and another consonant, double the end consonant.
  h**op** – hop**ped** – hop**ping**
     cvc
  st**ep** – step**ped** – step**ping**
     cvc

- Do not double *w* or *x*.
  snow – snow**ed** – snow**ing**
  mix – mix**ed** – mix**ing**

b Two-syllable verbs

- If the verb ends in a consonant, vowel, and another consonant, and the accent is on the first syllable of the word; do *not* double the end consonant.
  li**sten** – listen**ed** – listen**ing**
  o**ffer** – offer**ed** – offer**ing**

- If the verb ends in a consonant, vowel, and another consonant, and the accent is on the second syllable of the word; double the end consonant.
  per**mit** – permit**ted** – permit**ting**
  pre**fer** – prefer**red** – prefer**ring**

4 Should I write *ie* or *ei*?

This rhyme can help you remember whether to use *ie* or *ei*.

> *I* before *E* except after *C*
> or when sounded like *A*
> as in *neighbor* or *weigh*.

I before *E*:	believe, niece, relief
Except after *C*:	receive, deceive, conceit
Or when sounded like *A*:	eight, freight

Exceptions to this rule include *either, neither, height,* and *foreign*.

H Punctuation (P)

1 What punctuation do I need at the end of a sentence?

a Use a period at the end of a statement.

Today is Wednesday.

b Use a question mark at the end of a question.

Where are you going?

c Use an exclamation point to end a sentence with strong feeling.

I am very angry at you!

2 When do I need to use a *comma*?

a Use commas in a list of three or more things. Do not use a comma in a list of only two things.

She bought eggs, juice, milk, and bread at the store.
He laughed and cried.

b Use a comma after a transition (*then, also, next, after that,* etc.).

Then, he jumped through the window.

c In a compound sentence, put a comma after the first independent clause.

It started to rain, so we hurried inside.

d Use a comma in a complex sentence if the dependent clause comes first in the sentence.

While I was daydreaming, the teacher asked me a question.
    dependent clause   independent clause

e Do not use a comma if the dependent clause comes after the independent clause.

The teacher asked me a question while I was daydreaming.
    independent clause   dependent clause

3 When do I need to use an *apostrophe*?

a Use an apostrophe + -*s* to show possession. If the word ends in -*s,* add only an apostrophe.

> I saw <u>Ann's</u> new car yesterday.

> I saw the <u>boys'</u> new bikes yesterday.

b Do not use an apostrophe for the possessive form of *it.*

> The tree lost <u>its</u> leaves.

c Use an apostrophe to make a contraction.

> it's, there's, that's (contraction of *is*)

> can't, won't, wouldn't (contraction of *not*)

> she'll, I'll, that'll (contraction of *will*)

4 How do I use *quotation marks*?

When you tell a story, you often write words that people in the story say. When you do this, you must use quotation marks around those words.

Look at these examples. Notice where the periods, commas, question marks, exclamation points, and quotation marks are placed.

a Speaker's name first

> <u>Kelly</u> said, "Open the door."

b Speaker's name last

> "Open the door," said <u>Kelly</u>.

c Speaker's name in the middle of a sentence

> "Open the door," said <u>Kelly</u>, "or I will knock it down!"

d Speaker's name before or after two sentences

> <u>Kelly</u> said, "Open the door. If you don't, I will knock it down!"
> "Open the door. If you don't, I will knock it down!" said <u>Kelly</u>.

e Speaker's name in the middle of two sentences

> "Open the door," said <u>Kelly</u>. "If you don't, I will knock it down!"

▌ Capitalization (C)

1 What should I *capitalize*?

> **a** Capitalize the first word in every sentence.
>
> <u>Her</u> baby is beautiful.
> <u>The</u> night was dark.
>
> **b** Capitalize the pronoun *I*.
>
> My friend and <u>I</u> will wait here.
> <u>I</u> think that <u>I</u> will stay home tonight.
>
> | | | |
> |---|---|---|
> | **c** Names: | Susan Tuttle, Mark D. Wheaton | |
> | **d** Days: | Sunday, Monday, Tuesday | |
> | **e** Months: | January, February, March | |
> | **f** Holidays: | Valentine's Day, New Year's Day | |
> | **g** Nationalities: | Korean, Thai, Mexican | |
> | **h** Languages: | Chinese, English, Arabic | |
> | **i** Cities: | New York, Jakarta, Tokyo | |
> | **j** Countries: | Canada, Brazil, Australia | |
> | **k** Continents: | South America, Africa, Europe | |
> | **l** Names for deity: | God, Allah | |

2 What should I *not capitalize*?

> | | |
> |---|---|
> | **a** Seasons: | spring, summer, winter, fall (autumn) |
> | **b** Sports: | basketball, tennis, football |
> | **c** School subjects: | mathematics, biology, history |